CO-OPERATIVES IN AMERICA
Their Past, Present, and Future

Special Edition

PRINTED FOR

THE CO-OPERATIVE LEAGUE

OF THE U. S. A.

Co-operatives
IN AMERICA
Their Past, Present and Future

BY *Ellis Cowling*

WITH AN INTRODUCTION BY

J. P. WARBASSE

President of the Co-operative League of the U. S. A.

14587

COWARD-McCANN, INC.

New York 1938

This book is dedicated to Marion Brevier Cowling who helped her husband in every step of its preparation.

Acknowledgments

THE completion of this work would have been impossible without the help of friends.

I am indebted to the directors and manager of the Trumbull Farm Bureau Co-operative of Cortland, Ohio, for allowing me time enough from my regular duties to complete the writing.

Mr. A. W. Ricker, editor of the *Farmers Union Herald*, Mr. Thomas Cheek of the Oklahoma Farmers Union, Mr. L. S. Herron, editor of the *Nebraska Union Farmer*, Mr. Chester Graham of the Michigan Farmers Union, and especially Mrs. Gladys Talbott Edwards, Junior Leader of the National Farmers Union, gave invaluable aid in collecting material about Farmers Union Co-operatives.

Mr. Merlin Miller of the Consumers Co-operative Association of North Kansas City rendered a like service in providing information about the organization with which he is identified.

Dr. James Peter Warbasse of the Co-operative League of the U. S. A. and Mr. A. W. Warinner of the Central States Co-operative League loaned me valuable historical material on the American co-operative movement.

ACKNOWLEDGMENTS

I am grateful to Dr. David Sonquist of the Central States Co-operative League, to Mr. Anthony Lehner of the Pennsylvania Farm Bureau Co-operative Association, to Mr. Thomas Coward and his editorial staff for reading the manuscript and making many helpful suggestions for its improvement.

ELLIS COWLING

Introduction

CO-OPERATION in America is not new. It began among the animals that practiced mutual aid in their economic and social lives—in getting their food, and in protecting themselves from the elements and from their enemies. It continued among the primitive peoples of this continent, who did the same things in their different ways. The North American Indians organized themselves co-operatively and carried on their affairs in closer conformity to what are now called Rochdale methods than do many societies which are called co-operative today.

The Indians set up a tribal democracy in which each invested, as his contribution to share capital, his goods and his man power. They distributed to each member according to his needs. From distribution they moved back toward production. The chase, the forests, and the fields yielded food which was co-operatively apportioned. Each member got what he required and what in man power he paid for. No funds received interest, because no money was needed. The use of wampum was exceptional, and unnecessary within the tribe. Reserves, as a common surplus saving in the form of food, clothing, and other supplies, were built up to carry the tribe through the winter or other difficult season. The important fact was that all production and distribution were for service and not for private profit. Industry was not to make the difference between the cost and selling price by selling to somebody else.

In the strict meaning of the word this could not be called Rochdale co-operation. It was long before the Rochdale period. But it was the form of collectivism out of which Rochdale co-operation grew.

Were the high ethical standards of these people the result of these co-operative practices or did they practice co-operation because of their standards of ethics? Perhaps the latter is the case, and perhaps they employed the methods that are most natural. Certainly the co-operation of the Indians was most conducive to their preservation and survival. But when the white man with his individualistic, competitive, and acquisitive methods overwhelmed the Indians and coveted their property, he attempted to compel the Indians to adopt his ways. The Indians usually observed treaties; the white man broke them. When the Government put the Indians on isolated tribal lands, they continued with their co-operative methods and administered together their pooled possessions. Then followed a violation of their co-operative practices committed by the United States Government. An act was passed forbidding collective methods and compelling the splitting up of tribal property into small holdings for the individual Indians. Each Indian was made by law to own personally an individual piece of land. This was done at the behest of real estate speculators, white frontiersmen, and companies who desired to get the lands from the Indians. It was impossible to acquire the lands from the Indians while they were jointly held. But when each shareholder was compelled by law to take back his land capital into his own hands and its joint administration was broken up, the lone Indian was left at the mercy of unscrupulous forces which with the help of the Government, had little difficulty in robbing him of his property.

Now a new development is in process. The present Federal Government has appointed an Indian commissioner who not only knows the ethnology of the Indians but who understands co-operation also. Measures are on foot to restore to the Indians their ancient right to carry on their affairs co-operatively; they are also being taught the modern Rochdale methods and are being encouraged to apply these methods to their economic affairs. Honorable amends at last are offered for an old wrong.

The Mormons, when they settled in Utah, got from some source the collectivist idea. They organized and maintained a multitude of collective institutions which were co-operative in nature. They had a federation of their supply societies, which conducted a wholesale with a great warehouse in Salt

Lake City. This idea they probably acquired from the Indians and out of their own natural impulses as they strove for an ideal. Their co-operation was destroyed by their cupidity. When the possibilities of wealth and individual acquisitiveness were seen, the Mormons dropped their co-operative practices to give each individual the chance to acquire what he could. Some relics of the old co-operative tendency still survive, but in general this cult has committed itself to the profit economy of scarcity and individualistic acquisition. This means that a few are rich, but most are poor.

The many collectivist colonies that have developed in America also have exemplified some aspects of co-operation. The Shakers, dating back to 1787, practiced co-operative purchasing although they were essentially a productive and marketing enterprise. But they, like their many successors, had first in mind the consumers' philosophy. They were originally organized to be self-sufficient. They planned to produce most or all of the things they needed to consume. This is a fundamental concept of consumers' co-operation. Modern co-operation learns how to distribute first. But its members have capital which they have earned outside of the co-operative movement. The colonists had no other employment. They went to work together. They produced co-operatively together. They distributed co-operatively among themselves the products of their labor. They were co-operative consumers in the highest sense of the word. They neither bought nor sold for profit.

This was their ideal. But it was only an ideal. It lasted only during an initial stage. In time they found that they could produce more than they could consume. They sold the surplus. They made money. They got rich. They contracted the qualities of the capitalistic society by which they were surrounded. They caught the contagion from the very world from which they had hoped to escape. In the end, they divided their property among the individuals, and what was once an ideal and a successful business scheme came to an end. This has happened to a multitude of "co-operative colonies" which were set up in the United States during the first half of the past century. They are gone, with only their experience left to teach its lesson to those who may learn.

Among these colonies were New Lanark, the Amana Society, the Harmonists, the Bethel Commune, Brook Farm, and a hundred more—all ended largely because they departed from pure consumers' co-operation and went into profit business as marketing associations. There still survive a few old colonies practicing co-operation; but they are religious organizations and the members are held together by religious zeal. Such a one is the Huterisch Colony which adheres to the primitive Christianity. The few existing new colonies are apparently weak and temporary.

The American movement should have learned its lesson in the school of experience. It has made mistakes in some fields and it has been wisely guided in others. Co-operative societies in other countries likewise have suffered their mistakes. British co-operation has grown in a soil fertilized by as many casualities as occurred in America. But as serious and as costly as these experiences have been, they have been vastly less than the failures in profit business; and they continue to be less.

One co-operative principle has been generally observed in this country during the past twenty years. That is the principle of neutrality. American societies remain neutral in questions of politics and religion. They have no sides in politics nor do they endorse political candidates. As a result, the movement has not been split. American societies have on their boards of directors people of varying religious affiliations, people of all the leading political parties, and people of no religion and of no politics. In America, co-operation lives up to the highest co-operative possibilities in providing a common ground upon which all people may unite in harmony. American societies find strength in their neutrality.

This book which Mr. Cowling has written tells the story of co-operation in this country from about the Rochdale period. It begins with an honest recital of the mistakes and failures of the early movement. Bungling, errors, and failure in the early days were the rule. It might seem that co-operation had suffered staggering blows from which it could not recover. The setbacks might seem to represent irretrievable loss. But this is not the case. Every error taught its lesson. Co-operation, developing in the midst of a profit economy, is experimental. The American pioneers went to the school of trial and error. We now know their mistakes. We know how to avoid them. The pioneers paid the price; we are reaping the advantage.

In our American soil, fertilized by the blood and the dead bodies of a thousand societies, is now growing a movement enriched and nourished by the experiences of the past. We should not blame these pioneers. We owe them our gratitude and homage. They had little to guide them; we have much.

This book is a fair and clear picture also of the success into which American co-operation is growing. It is factual, and its philosophy is sound. It is a help to the understanding of this expanding movement, which on the whole is still much misunderstood. Those who entertain the idea that labor, organized as producers, can solve the problems of society, or even the problems of the working class, need the enlightenment which this book provides. The new economics is under obligations to Mr. Cowling for this lucid exposition of the co-operative method of business, now well advanced in America.

J. P. WARBASSE.

Contents

CO-OPERATIVES IN AMERICA
Their Past, Present, and Future

CHAPTER I

Three Englishmen
Upset a World

CHANGE IS IN THE SADDLE. No one can look at the past decade of American life and not be impressed with that fact. The years previous to 1929 saw the nation's business spiraling to the peak of a dizzy paper prosperity. Men talked of a new era when poverty would be abolished forever. The Republicanism of Coolidge and Mellon was looked upon as the last word in government. Here and there voices did speak of growing insecurity among laborers and increasing farm tenancy. But no one listened. The ears of the nation were tuned to other things.

Then the stock market crashed. The price of securities hit a toboggan. Business activity followed. The great productive and distributive machinery of America slowed down. Millions lost their jobs virtually over night. Want stalked a land whose citizens prated about overproduction.

Came the second Tuesday of November 1932. The people who had so enthusiastically elected "the great engineer" in 1928 emphatically repudiated him at the polls. The man who talked of "a New Deal" was swept into power. When the day for his inauguration was at hand the banking structure of the nation collapsed. The savings of millions were lost in the debris. Spurred on by a new executive and an applauding people, Congress passed a whole ream of new regulations for business and industry. NRA, AAA, TVA, CWA, PWA gave the alphabet a new significance for Americans. The coffers of the federal government were opened to feed the hungry and minister to a prostrate agriculture.

Four years passed. The Democratic party, after decades of experience as a minority group, found itself more firmly entrenched in power than any party had been for half a century. When the election returns were in, even the staid and conservative Supreme Court astonished the country by a complete reversal of its attitudes on governmental regulation of economic affairs.

Other things were happening. The United States —famous for being the great open-shop country of the world—witnessed a great stirring among its laboring classes. Unions were formed where they had been undreamed of before. Under the leadership of John L. Lewis the workers of the great mass-production industries—automobiles, steel, rubber, textiles—began to organize. The "sit down" strike was imported from France.

Detroit, automobile capital of the world, became the scene of a great struggle on the part of labor for the right to bargain collectively. Two of the

4

three big automobile makers recognized the unions. Big Steel gave in without a struggle. Unionism grew apace.

In the midst of the turmoil the wheels of industry started again. Factory production schedules crept upward toward the marks of 1929 and then surpassed them. Prosperity seemed about at hand. Yet lurking in the background were the millions still dependent upon their government for bread. In the closing months of 1937 business declined again. For a second time in a decade the economic machine stalled.

Not only America, but the whole world is in the grip of a great flux. Human affairs are changing. Civil wars, riots, bloodshed, war, and preparation for war bear witness.

Men react to the situation in many ways. Some long for the peace of their yesterdays. Millions drift —content to snatch the pleasures the present gives —unmindful of the past and heedless of the future. Some believe they are witnessing the birth pangs of a new and better order of human affairs. Others see only a swiftly approaching chaos. Multitudes are confused.

Past historians have been much concerned with the doings of politicians and potentates, whom they regarded as the determiners of human destiny. Modern historians have come to see that kings and governments are more symptoms and results than causes. Political rulers are pawns moved about by larger and more significant forces. Those who would have insight into human affairs must probe beneath the froth of politics and examine the realities of common life. The way men make their living is the most important single fact about the character of a civilization.

But all too few recognize that back of the present political changes and the unrest which stirs the world lies one great cause. For nearly two centuries men have been changing their method of wresting food, shelter, and clothing from the earth. We are in the grip of a revolution—not basically political, but industrial. There is a new factor in the human equation. That factor is *machine production*. This revolution was started by the enterprising English in the eighteenth century and has gone forward at an accelerating pace. And the end is not yet. James Hargreaves, Richard Arkwright, and James Watt —a weaver, a barber, and an engineer—set it in motion.

The weaver was evidently lazy, for he was forever trying to discover means of getting out of work. He spun and wove enough to make a living but devoted much of his time to figuring out ways of making one motion do the work of two. The first result of his endless tinkering was a system of pulleys by which he could join two carding combs and exactly halve the time necessary for carding a fleece

6

of wool. The efficiency of this simple device gave him added time for inventing. In 1762 he built a carding engine for a calico printer named Robert Peel. Peel saw possibilities in Hargreaves. He subsidized him as he devised things to make work easier.

Eventually he perfected a "Spinning Jenny"—named after Hargreaves' wife—which multiplied by eight the amount of thread which could be turned out by a single spinner. Fellow-workers regarded this new creation as "unfair competition." They broke into the inventor's home and smashed the machine. But they failed to destroy the idea. Hargreaves moved to a more tolerant community and proceeded to create a whole new set of problems for hand spinners by building a spinning mill, in 1768 at Nottingham.

Ten years later he died, little realizing that he had started a profound change in human affairs which historians would some day call "The Industrial Revolution."

Richard Arkwright was first a barber. Then he amassed a modest fortune as a mixer and merchant of hair dye. He has gone down in history as a great inventor. In 1767 he set to work to perfect cotton spinning machinery. He created the spinning mule. In 1771 he built a large factory at Cromford, in Derbyshire. The machinery in it was ingeniously devised and arranged with an eye to convenience and efficiency. He divided the labor among his employees so as to secure maximum production per man. He was the father of the factory system with its specialization and minute division of labor.

Arkwright's mill was run by water power. It remained for the third of the trio to give the factory system flexibility. He divorced it from its dependence upon falling water as a source of power.

The story of ...es Watt's perfecting of the steam engi.. .amiliar to every school boy. A contempo..ry of Hargreaves and Arkwright, his work fitted beautifully with theirs to complete the pattern of industrial change. In 1790 a Watt engine was set to work driving the machinery of an Arkwright factory. Thus the machine age was born.

The succeeding years have witnessed the progressive application of machinery, power, and the factory system to the production of goods. The machine has replaced human hands; the steam engine and electric motor, the energy of the human body. Men once *made* goods with the use of simple tools; they now *tend* the machines which do the work. This development has progressively enveloped the industrial world. Even agriculture, last of the great industries to be affected, is today a changed occupation. The hoe, the sickle, the flail are all but forgotten instruments. The gang plow, the four-row cultivator, the combine, and the tractor have relegated them to the museums. Tending machines is occupying an increasing portion of the farmer's time.

The change to machine production upset a thousand equations: cut the race loose from moorings ancient as history. Previous to the work of Hargreaves, Arkwright, and Watt, industry was largely carried on in the home. The muscles of men or animals presented the chief source of productive power. Tools there were, but they simply increased the productive efficiency of muscular energy. Changes in the social structure—from slavery to feudalism to free labor—did nothing to disturb man's basic dependence on his own physical strength. They were simply varying means of controlling human labor and distributing the results of it. The advent of the machine did disturb this dependence.

Hargreaves' spinning jenny was hand driven, but when Arkwright used water power to turn the spindles and Watt made possible the use of steam power there was something different under the sun. New and untiring giants were put to work doing what man had always done with his own strength. Man was pygmied by these Goliaths. Human hands could not compete with them. Industry moved from home to factory. The ownership of machines became the fulcrum by which a new class raised itself to economic and political power. Those who could not own were given a single choice—tend machines or starve. The stomach is a tremendous factor in human affairs: they chose to tend machines.

For one hundred and fifty years mankind has been trying to adjust itself to this profound change in its sources and uses of energy. These years have inevitably been characterized by heaving turmoil.

This turmoil was started by the workers who saw in the machine a threat against their independence and security. The rioting spinners who destroyed Hargreaves' first machines were reacting blindly to the danger they did not fully understand. If they could have foreseen the events of succeeding decades they might have been more violent in their reaction. The replacement of men by machines has put on the backs of common folk a constant burden of making occupational changes. Whole trades, such as that of glass blower and carriage maker, have been wiped out, and those trained in them forced to find other means of earning their living. Over every occupation hangs the constant threat that the inventor's genius may make today's job unnecessary tomorrow. A new process or product may make the very thing produced obsolete and inefficient. So long as this is true there can be no security for those who have only the labor of their hands to exchange for bread.

Strikes, bread riots, hunger marches, trade unions, farm holidays, labor political parties are but expressions of the demand of those who cannot own machines for a measure of security. Violent protests will continue, and probably increase in virulence, until human society has learned to use machines in a manner which will bring respite from present strains and burdens.

It is doubtful indeed if the three men who started us into the machine age dreamed of the vast changes which were about to be ushered into the world. They seem to have been interested only in immediate and contemporary problems. Perhaps they had visions of great abundance for the human race and a new freedom from the scarcity which dependence on human energy had made inescapable.

But the machine age arrived with the triumph of the idea of individualism. The Middle Ages are often called the "dark ages." Unquestionably life did move at a leisurely pace and much of it was drab and dreary. However, it was characterized by a certain sense of social solidarity which made life bearable. The division of land and labor on the medieval manor did give a rough equality of access to the store of material wealth—meager as it was. There was a rather complete sharing of whatever of abundance or scarcity fell to the lot of the community. Within the cities the guilds fostered a sense of interdependence. Guild law required that men look after one another. Guild regulation saw to it that no man grabbed too big a share of wealth for himself.

The decay of feudalism brought all these things to an end. Men became individualists in their religion and in their business. Regulation of economic practices came to be regarded as old fashioned and outmoded.

It was just at the dawn of the machine age that Adam Smith published his *Wealth of the Nations*— bible of the cult which says that every businessman should do that which is right in his own eyes. It was his contention that business and industry should be wholly without governmental regulation. He was no believer in the benevolence of the trading class. He was committed to the idea that every man was out to make all he could for himself. Service to society was rendered solely for the purpose of accumulating private profits. But he felt that the best way to prevent exploitation of the public by these classes was to have free and unfettered competition. He believed that government regulation usually served the private interest of special groups much better than it did the public good. He suspected the motives of politicians as much as he did those of industrialists and traders. The eighteenth century witnessed the triumph of his ideas. A large portion of the time of the English parliament during the years from 1760 to 1800 was spent in repealing medieval laws regulating commerce and industry. Every man was left to do that which was to his greatest personal advantage in the very hour when machinery presented humanity with a new set of problems which needed the attention of the best collective intelligence of the race. The development

machine production was left entirely in the hands
those who saw in this new technique only a method
amassing great wealth for themselves. The result
been untold suffering on the part of those whose
verty has forced them to sell the skill of their
ands for whatever machine owners were willing to
y.

Despite the fact that the growth of this new tech-
ique of production has been accompanied by much
edless human misery, few intelligent people want
go back to the former dependence on hand labor.
ahatma Gandhi of India has gained some pub-
ity by talking of a return to the conditions of the
e-machine age. But his philosophy has no appeal
r the American mind.

The average American is very much in love with
e mechanical gadgets of our industrial civilization.
he growth of invention has been intimately linked
ith our national history. We make heroes of our
ientists and inventors. Nations have worshiped
ose who served them worse.

We love machines for what they will do for us
—for the comforts they produce, for the drudgery
hich they save, for their efficiency in producing the
ecessities which sustain life and the luxuries which
nrich it. They have made our thunderous cities pos-
ible and freed us from a thousand natural terrors.

In 19 6 when a great drouth destroyed the entire
arvest f many parts of our nation, famine did not

follow. Food poured into the stricken areas ov
transportation system dependent on a thousand
tricate mechanisms for its proper functioning. 7
centuries before would have seen death and sta
tion sweeping across the land.

When the Ohio valley was swept by a delug
1937 there was a remarkably low loss of life. C
alties were counted in tens, not thousands. The p
lation moved out ahead of the water by motor b
truck, train, and airplane. Radios hurled warni
through the ether and co-ordinated the work of
rescue parties. Without these, whole cities wo
probably have seen the mud left in streets
houses made ghastly fertile with the bodies of th
citizens. It did not happen because of machin
Flood and famine are great terrors only in th
countries which have despised or never heard of
inventor's genius.

We will not repudiate the machines. They are
too useful. We love to be served by them. Like
entire human race, we are inherently lazy. We w
only because we must. History proves how little m
really care for labor. No leisure class has ever volu
tarily given up its right to loaf. Every leisure cla
when threatened, has defended with violence t
privilege of living without working. However mu
lip service is paid to the virtue of industry, tho
who have been able to escape labor by own ng slav
or serfs or clipping coupons have regard ed h

work as a habit not intended for personal practice. In spite of all the problems that they have brought we will not cease loving to have our work done by giants of steel. Why should we?

One hundred and fifty years of industrialism is not to be repudiated. But an ever increasing number demand respite from the insecurity which is a part of life today. Natural disasters such as drouth, unprecedented cold, floods have lost many of their terrors, but haunting fears of loss of employment, of facing old age without resources, of loss of home or land have taken their place.

In an effort to rid themselves of these new enemies of human well-being, the race is experimenting with new forms of social and political organization. Three of these—Fascism, Socialism, and Communism—enjoy the greatest publicity.

Fascism is an effort to freeze civilization into stability by force. It attempts to preserve *as is* the inequalities and injustices of the present situation. It turns the direction of national affairs over to a small clique headed by a dictator. That clique tells others what they can and cannot do. It does away with political parties; it stops industrial strife by forbidding strikes; it stops discussion of economic and social problems by curtailing freedom of the press, free speech, and free assembly. It distracts the attention of the masses from their bread-and-butter problems by dragging out the brass bands, the flags, by creating parades, by patriotic and nationalistic oratory. Those who refuse to be distracted are clubbed into silence.

Countries under Fascism have a peace of a kind. In part it is peace born of fear to voice any but the *approved* opinion. It is in part the peace that comes from an intense sense of belonging to and serving with fanatical devotion something bigger than one's self. Its setting up of the state as a god to be served with complete and self-effacing devotion has brought some of the comfort that dogmatic religion always gives. But Fascism utterly fails to harness machines to the task of enriching human life. It cannot permanently work because it leaves untouched the basic causes of our present unrest. It may succeed in temporarily hypnotizing the people of a distraught country but it leaves their basic problems unsolved. Its constant appeal to national grandeur and to military adventure is a terrible sowing of the dragon's teeth.

Communism and Socialism call for a drastic reorganization of society—particularly of its property relationships. They would substitute collective ownership for private ownership and use the government as a means of making the change. They alike call on the disinherited workers to organize themselves for ownership of our industrial machinery. When the people own them, machines will be put to work serving all.

They differ seriously in the methods by which they propose to reach this end. Communism, like Fascism, relies strongly on dictatorship and violence.

The Communists say the successful winning of a violent class war is the first step toward bringing peace and security to mankind. They ask the disinherited to unite in a single great army, capable of seizing power in a revolution. They point to Russia as the great example of the successful use of their method. No one can deny that the Communists did wage successful war against the rulers of Tsarist Russia. They did it because they won the sympathy of that nation's armed forces. They capitalized the Russian soldier's thorough disgust with the World War. He had had his fill of death and mud and cooties and was glad enough to take it out on those who had forced such things on him. Even Trotsky admits that conditions were just right for the successful use of the Communistic method. He further admits that their success was largely dependent on the insight of Lenin who guessed right as to when violence would work. Had he guessed wrong, it might have been another story.

The Communists invite to a great gamble. On the surface their program has a direct and ruthless simplicity. They decree death to the owning class. Death has a complete and inescapable finality. Yet when all the complications are considered—the necessity of controlling armed forces, of guessing the right moment for direct action, of waiting for the day when conditions are properly ripe for success—the semblance of simplicity disappears. The Communists boast of the certainty of their method. Its very uncertainty is its chief practical weakness.

Communism will appeal to the irresponsible and the desperate. Those who have lost their last piece of land or their last opportunity for securing subsistence wages may embrace it. The rest will have little stomach for risking their small stake in the present for the uncertainties of civil war.

Socialism repudiates Communism's trust in violence—except, perhaps, as a last resort, in case force is used in an attempt to defeat its program. The Socialist believes in democratic processes. He seeks to create the will to own in the disinherited, and to organize that will behind a vigorous and vigilant political party. When that party wins control of the forces of government then it will take over for the people the basic industries of the country. It will make these the property of the political state which will operate them for the good of all.

The proposal is simple enough, but those who advocate it have one serious blind spot for a fact of human history: politicians are inevitably controlled by property. Without regard for political belief or creed, political rulers are subservient to those who own the wealth of a nation. Political power is the result of economic power. The winning of an election

18

is an empty victory for those who have no possessions. The Socialists have won elections and become heads of governments—in Germany, in England, in certain cities in the United States—but there has followed no sweeping reorganization of property relationships. The people have not become the owners of the industries of those nations or those cities. The government did not take control and administer the basic industries for the good of all. It attempted minor reforms and the correction of certain abuses, but little more.

There is little evidence that any large group of American people are interested in any of these three programs. Certainly neither the Communist nor the Socialist groups have had any remarkable growth during the great depression. The average American has an ingrained distrust of politicians which makes him shy at the idea of the government owning and controlling any large portion of industry. There is within his breast a love of doing and saying what he pleases, which creates considerable immunity to Fascism and Communism. Jittery people see tendencies in both directions and constantly raise the cry of "Wolf! Wolf!" but an increasing number respond to these alarms with a yawn.

If there is any one thing to which the American people are turning as a means of solving the problems which industrialism has created, it is to "collective bargaining." The rapid growth of labor unions, first under the spur of the collective bargaining clause of the National Recovery Act and more recently under the generalship of John L. Lewis and his Committee for Industrial Organization, bears its own evidence to this fact.

The great mass production industries—automobiles, steel, rubber—have each in turn been assaulted by the wave of unionization. Back of the movement lies the idea that since capital is organized to bargain collectively, labor must be also. By demanding shorter hours and better wages and by securing the right to bargain for these things as a group, labor has hopes of eliminating many of the uncertainties and insecurities now oppressing it. Many of the more enlightened industrial magnates have, with some reluctance, come to accept unionization as a necessary part of a changing world. Our liberal newspapers and journals have proclaimed this wave of interest in labor organization as a great turning point in our social and industrial life. Congress, through the Wagner Labor Relations Act, has said that men have a right, when they so desire, to be unhampered in their purpose to sell the labor of their hands collectively. The Supreme Court has declared that the founding fathers of our federal constitution did not deny men this privilege. Many Socialists, losing faith in the political future of their party, have turned to this newly-born labor movement as the great hope for the common man's tomorrow.

However, this emphasis on labor organization may be regarded by our future historians as just another evidence of our failure to realize that an industrial revolution has taken place which is to an increasing degree replacing hand labor with mechanical tools of production. The organization of labor is the organization of a force which is destined to have less and less significance in human affairs. The industrial revolution first rendered useless the hand tools of laborers. Today the need for hands gradually disappears.

Our inventors are still busy making machinery more automatic. The attainment of 1929 production schedules in 1937 without the absorption of many millions of the unemployed is but an indication of industry's lessening need for human beings in its productive processes.

Our infatuation with labor organization is not the only evidence of our refusal to recognize that we are living in an age of machines. The dealings of the government with the unemployed reflect a like blindness to economic facts. It has created agencies such as the CWA and the WPA to give work to those without it. But in so doing it has regarded the machine as a plague. It has not placed men at work with the most efficient tools the age affords for the purpose of making them as useful as possible in creating new goods for human consumption and enjoyment. Rather it has kept men busy with the aged pick and shovel. It encouraged inefficiency just because public opinion somehow wants to associate the putting in of hours of drudgery with the right to consume goods. That association is a hang-over from the days when the inefficiency of hand production made back-breaking toil necessary for human survival.

The tendency of many to regard unemployment as the basic problem of our age is another case in point. Men refuse to recognize the fact that the race has gone so far in solving its production problems that the necessity for human drudgery is vanishing with the hoe and sickle. There will be increasing *unemployment* at productive tasks in the future. Only a death sentence for every inventor of labor-saving machinery can prevent that. There will be less work to do. What we have to decide is whether or not the work that does need doing shall be distributed among all the able bodied of the nation with adequate distribution of consumers' goods to all. We can, of course, continue the present situation in which many at both ends of the social scale live in idleness while those who are so unfortunate as to be poor, as well as idle, eke out an existence on some sort of dole. The problem of *unemployment,* as we know it now, will disappear when men tackle the problem of proper distribution of consumers' goods.

The labor problem is not the fundamental issue. The right to bargain collectively for wages and hours does not touch the basic need for abundant consumption. The careful studies of the conservative Brookings Institute should prove to every skeptic that if America were exploiting her own capacity to produce, poverty could be ended. America is not exploiting her capacity to produce because the present system of distribution has bottle-necked the process. There will come release for the masses from insecurity and uncertainty only when we cease being engrossed with the problems of the producer alone and give time and attention to the interests of the consumer.

Collective bargaining for higher wages and shorter hours appears to be a way of increasing consumption. It does enable those who work to get better wages, but so long as the owners of industry can pass on higher labor costs to the consumer in higher prices nothing has happened. The workers may handle more money in the course of a year but more money in itself does not mean greater purchasing power. It does not mean enlarged access to the great reservoirs of goods which we can turn out with our present productive facilities.

There must be something more than unionization of labor. Working for that alone is as futile as fussing around with the pumps and storage tanks of a city water system whose mains, lead-in lines, and house plumbing have failed. If we solve the pressing problems of our age it will be because we become concerned with the building of a new system of distribution.

Those whom the machine age has disinherited must acquire the ownership of the stores, the wholesales, and the productive machinery which makes and distributes goods. There must be organization of the consumers toward that end.

Fortunately we do not have to forge the techniques for giving such ownership to the people today. Others who have gone before us have shown the way. Over a century ago some of those whom the industrial revolution had deprived of ownership of the tools of production began experimentation with consumer ownership. Out of their trials and errors, and eventually their successes, was born the Consumers Co-operative movement—a method by which millions the world round are becoming owners both of machines and the channels of distribution through which goods are placed in their hands. However, they are not achieving ownership as workers, as producers. They are achieving it as consumers. There is a difference.

For an understanding of this movement and its technique of organizing business we must retrace some history. We must first visit nineteenth-century England.

CHAPTER II

A Prophet In the Land

THE FIRST REACTIONS to the Industrial Revolution were almost wholly instinctive and unreasoned. Workers saw in the factories only a threat against their livelihood. Some organized themselves into machine destroying mobs. Industrialists saw a golden chance to make profits. The world was hungry for goods. Machines offered a chance to satisfy that hunger—for a price. The lust for wealth drove those who could afford it to build factories, and hire, for as little as possible, the laborers whose hand-production was rendered obsolete.

This meant misery and squalor. The slums arrived with the factory. England became a land of deserted villages—vividly described by Goldsmith—and factory towns, where poverty stalked the streets. Before many years had passed owners made a discovery: the nimble fingers of little children could tend whirling spindles and power looms. Child labor began. Men and women lived in idleness, supported by their little ones. Or else the whole family was put to work to secure a pittance that kept body and soul together on a plane that could not be called a healthy animal existence. Human flesh was cheap.

The owners of industry did not care. They were interested in the golden stream that flowed into their coffers. Riches and misery grew side by side—parts of the same sordid story.

But every action brings its reaction. In the mind of a man named Robert Owen came the first prophetic revulsion against this heartless exploitation. He realized that humanity had a new factor with which to deal; he foresaw the tremendous changes which new methods of production would bring in human affairs. He believed that those changes could be intelligently guided into constructive channels. He felt that the new misery and the new wealth were not necessarily bound together. Only blindness and irresponsibility kept them so. He saw in the machine a productive instrument capable of blessing all whom it affected. He had faith that the factory system could be reformed, and a quality rare in men—willingness to have reform begin with himself.

Owen was an owner of machines and a good businessman—in the usual meaning of the term. At eighteen he controlled a half interest in a factory employing forty workers. He made his start on five hundred dollars of borrowed money, and sold out at the end of one year at a substantial profit. At nineteen he was a factory manager in Manchester. So well did he handle the force of five hundred people who worked under him that he was given a partnership in the business. Shortly thereafter he sold out again and became manager and partner in the New Lanark Mills.

Here between two and three thousand men, women, and children lived and worked under typical conditions of poverty and filth. The hours of labor for all hands were from six in the morning until seven at night. Parents brought their children to work after their seventh year. Nearly five hundred orphans from nearby work-houses were there under the despotic rule of factory management. Owen's biographer describes conditions thus: "Deep poverty drove the workers to the mills from the cities; and the work-house authorities gladly—to get rid of them—sent a cartload of orphans, aged six and seven, now and again. The general character may be deduced. Their homes were foul. Their habits primitive. Their streets were sewers. The public houses were infamous. Thieving, lying, swearing, drinking, and fighting were as common as the squalor with which they spattered the golden valley"—of the Clyde.

Owen spent fifteen years remaking New Lanark. In 1800 he quietly resolved that poverty, destitution, and ignorance would not be by-products of the excellent cotton goods he was producing. He did everything that a benevolent capitalist could do: cut the hours of labor, put the children in school at the expense of the mills, paid wages that made decent living possible, cleaned up the streets, established company stores that sold excellent goods at reasonable prices. New Lanark became a model factory town, known all over Europe for being the one bright spot in terrible industrial dreariness. The workers responded to kindness and justice. They changed with their environment.

But Owen had partners to deal with. They tolerated his fantastic ideas only because he produced fat dividends even while spending money on these unheard-of efforts to transform factory working conditions. Eventually, however, their love of profits caused them to interfere. They reasoned that returns might have been even greater had there been none of this social experimentation. By 1809 the first set of associates had become disgusted and sold out—at a handsome profit. In 1811 the second group complained like the first and only with the help of rich and public-spirited Quakers was Owen able to keep control of his beloved community. With some help and some hindrance from them he continued with his experiment until 1816. By that time the results were so unmistakable that he believed the hour was at hand to publicize them before the world.

He felt that he had found a way by which society could be transformed. His formula included universal education, elimination of child labor, reduction of working hours for adults to ten per day, the institution of public works to absorb those who could

not find employment in private industry, the abolition of religious intolerance and war, drastic revision
of the criminal code, and basic reformation of jails
and the administration of justice—a program not
dissimilar to parts of our New Deal.

He made his first appeal to his own class—the
factory owners. He simply asked that they do what
his success at New Lanark proved could be done.
Later he asked his government to sponsor his program. The owners of industry saw in his schemes
only a serious interference with profits. Officehold-
ers were more inclined to give the matter serious
consideration, but in the face of the hostility of the
industrialists, they would do nothing. Owen's appeal
fell on deaf ears. The real and nominal rulers of
a great nation were little interested in lessening the
blow which the invention of machinery had struck
against the peace and security of common folk. They
were interested only in profits and in their own political careers.

Then came the end of the Napoleonic wars. Peace
came to Europe after long and bitter struggles
against the France of the first Napoleon. Peace
brought its turmoil. The usual post-war business
reaction set in. Unemployment stalked the land.
Wages were forced down. Misery increased. Owen
saw that war and killing had increased business
profits, brought a kind of feverish prosperity, while
peace brought poverty and deprivation for thou-

sands upon thousands. He pondered the fact and began to wonder if a business system that thrived in war and languished in peace could be anything but rotten at its core.

The increased suffering of the masses resulted in strikes, hunger marches, and riots. The government which had refused to consider Owen's reform program was willing to resort to ruthless violence to quell the rioting of hungry men—and did.

Owen watched the events of these troubled years with growing disillusionment. He lost all hope of getting favorable consideration of his plans from those in high places. Love of money rather than love of men was too deeply rooted in the hearts of factory owners for them to take Owen's appeal seriously. He saw that changes would have to come by other methods than those he first considered workable. The importance of restoring ownership to those who had lost their property slowly dawned on him. He gradually came to think in terms of what factory workers could do for themselves rather than what he could get others to do for them.

He clearly saw that individualistic ownership of the tools of production was out of the question, so far as the laborers were concerned, under the factory system. Collective ownership alone seemed possible. With heroic abandonment he set himself to the task of making the workers owners of their factories. He financed workers' colonies in which there was social ownership of land and factories. In these colonies he established democratic control and constantly emphasized the ideal of working together for common good. But his "Villages of Co-operation and Union" failed. Owen had too great faith in the inherent goodness of human nature. He did not realize how completely the dominant spirit of individualism had rendered men incapable of intelligent social action. Medieval habits of communal living had been too long forgotten to be easily revived. Then, too, the problems of factory production, labor management, and profitable sale of things produced were too complex for the workers to handle. They were utterly without administrative experience and without a schoolmaster to train them.

One of those colonies was established on American soil. New Harmony, Indiana, was Owen's New World experiment. It went the same route taken by the Old World efforts. Failure was the common end. All these attempts served only to demonstrate that ownership could not be *given* to the people. They must claim it for themselves.

While the colonies were failing, the disinherited workers were beginning to do things for themselves. Trade Unionism slowly got under way against the combined hostility of industry and government. Owen gave his blessing to the movement. He helped form the Grand National Trades Union of Great Britain and Ireland—a federation of labor unions.

Within six months the organization was suppressed. But it was a beginning. The victims of machine production had begun to demand a voice in their own destiny.

Until his death in 1858 this man gave every encouragement to the workers to organize themselves: into trade unions for securing better wages and working conditions; into little productive societies in which there was common ownership of a small factory or workshop. Following a builders' strike in Birmingham in 1833 he even recommended that they organize their own stores so that they could have control over sources of food and household necessities. He saw that the organized strength of the weak might, if rightly directed, become a sure defense against the heartlessness of the mighty.

Owen died a poor man. He had spent a fortune in an effort to solve a problem which was too big for him. Years of talking, writing, and lavish expenditure of funds yielded but very meager results. His dreams were unfulfilled. Judged by ordinary standards he died a failure.

He takes no place in history for his practical accomplishments. He is honored because he was the first to attempt to deal intelligently with the problems which the coming of machine production has created for the human race. He made the mistakes any beginner would have made. It is not surprising that he failed to do anything more than focus attention on the major issues. We are deeply indebted to him for starting men in search of a solution. He did demonstrate that squalor and human wretchedness were not necessarily a part of the industrial picture.

The evolution of his thinking is interesting for us. He first tried to change the world by example. New Lanark was his great illustration of what could be done in an industrial hell. He found that most men were not even interested in what he had accomplished. He started out with a simple faith in the goodness of governments and in the possibilities of the political method of solving social problems. He discovered that the welfare of men without property is not a very serious concern of the state. He came to see that only those who are adversely affected by bad conditions will give sustained support to a program of changing them. He sensed the importance of property ownership in the affairs of men and advocated that those who are too poor to own property individually pool their resources and own together. His final belief was that when men discovered how to own together they would have in their hands the key to their own destiny.

Owen did not show how it could be done. It remained for others, more lowly in wealth and culture than he, to perfect a method by which men of poverty could quietly and yet successfully make themselves men of property.

CHAPTER III

Revolution In a Grocery Store

THE FOURTH DECADE of the past century has been nick-named "the hungry forties." The western world was enjoying one of the periodic business depressions which have been an ever recurring affliction during one hundred and fifty years of expanding industrialism. Political upheavals, bread riots, strikes, unemployment, suffering, were all a part of the history of that time. Factory workers and small farmers were facing difficult problems. For upon them, as usual, fell the heaviest burdens of want and privation. There was no government relief or unemployment insurance to dull the edge of their suffering. Many had no work; those who did found wages cut to the bone. They were troubled years.

One of the groups particularly hard hit were the flannel weavers of a city of north England, called Rochdale. Desperation drove them to a strike in 1843. The strikers faced all the difficulties involved in trying to get higher wages in a day when the labor market is glutted with those who have no work. It was inevitable that the strike fail. Nor were the factory owners slow to take advantage of its collapse. When others went back to work those who led the walkout found that their services were no longer desired. All the factories of the city boycotted them; a black list of such trouble makers had been prepared and circulated effectively.

The loss of that strike was to them tragedy indeed. It meant the eclipse of their hope for better living conditions. It meant the deepening of a misery that was already more than they felt able to bear. But out of their loss was born the technique that Robert Owen had failed to discover. The black-listed strike leaders of Rochdale found a way by which they could make themselves men of property.

It was in part the result of seeds Owen had planted. Some of these men had heard of his idea of workers owning property together. They had dreamed dreams of worker-ownership of mills and factories. Even before the strike they had experimented and failed in attempting to own their own stores.

Talk was one thing these men could afford. They spent long hours discussing their problems and wondering what they could do by way of self-deliverance. It was one way of making their lot more bearable. Eventually from their conversation grew a conviction: the way out was to go into business for themselves.

Out of that conviction grew an organization. They called it the "Equitable Society of Rochdale Pioneers." Their basic purpose was to make themselves their own employers. With pathetic courage they stated the ambitious objectives of their association in the following language:

"The establishment of a store for the sale of provisions, clothing, etc.

"The building, purchasing, or erecting of a number of houses in which those members, desiring to assist each other in improving their domestic and social conditions, may reside.

"The manufacture of such articles as the society may determine upon, to provide employment of such members who may be without employment, or who may be suffering in consequence of repeated reduction in their wages.

"The purchasing, or renting of an estate or estates of land, which shall be cultivated by members who may be out of employment, or whose labor is badly remunerated.

"And further: that as soon as practicable this society shall proceed to arrange powers of production, distribution, education, and government—or, in other words, to establish a self-supporting home colony of united interests, or assist other societies in establishing such colonies."

Whatever they may have lacked in resources, the Rochdale Pioneers certainly had no lack of ambition. They were boldly proclaiming their intention of solving problems that had given pause to Robert Owen with all his wealth, and which had baffled the

36

statesmen of Europe. They were out to take possession of the earth: to become owners of stores, manufacturing enterprises, land, educational institutions, and government. They would become men of property.

In the beginning there were twenty-eight members of this seemingly mad society—about to do battle with the giants of a lusty young industrial capitalism. One woman was among the company. Her name was Ann Tweedale.

The Pioneers started their ambitious schemes in a most unspectacular manner. They began by saving money. It was a slow, painful process for there was little money on which they could lay their hands. It was about all they could do to keep body and soul together. But they got a halfpenny here and a two-pence there. Halfpennies and twopences will eventually add up into shillings, and shillings into pounds. At the end of a year they had twenty-eight English pounds: $140 in American money. It wasn't much, but they believed it to be enough to take the first step in their plan.

A store was opened in an old warehouse basement on Toad Lane on the night of December 21, 1844. Its meager stock could have been hauled home in one large wheelbarrow. It consisted of sugar, oatmeal, flour, butter, and candles. The total value was $70. When the shutters were taken down for the opening, rowdy street urchins shouted their derision. The "ow'd weavers' shop" wasn't much of a store. In the beginning it was open for business two nights a week and the clerking was done by unpaid volunteers.

It was many months before the business was large enough to justify its staying open for six days in the week with a full time manager in charge but eventually that day came. The store grew as if it had within itself something of the strange power of a fertilized cell to grow into an active self-directing organism. At the end of the first year the membership had grown to seventy-four; the capital to $900. The first annual report contained the cheerful news that $3,500 had trickled across the counter and a net saving of $160 achieved.

Robert Owen passed away in 1858, probably without ever having heard of the Rochdale society. But three years later its membership totaled two thousand families, and the capital $75,000. When the golden jubilee of the opening of the store was celebrated in 1894, membership was twelve thousand and the annual volume of business $1,500,000.

The Pioneers were not only great dreamers; they were also successful businessmen. Success did not come, however, without some difficulties. As early as 1850 a crisis developed which all but carried their venture down the road which Owen's co-operative villages had taken. Mild achievement brought ambitions for expansion, so at the turn of the half-century the society decided to buy a flour mill. It looked like a means of taking them one step further into the program they had cut out for themselves. However, they failed to take account of all the factors involved.

First, it is one thing to manufacture a product: it is another to market it. The mill made much more flour than the store needed to supply its customers and it wasn't an easy matter to dispose of the surplus. Private merchants weren't overly eager to buy from an organization maintaining a retail outlet in competition with them. Second, people do not always like what is good for them. The Pioneers resolved in the very beginning to handle only good quality products which were neither doctored nor adulterated. The flour which the mill produced was slightly yellow—as is all unbleached flour. But the housewives of Rochdale had bought flour bleached with alum for so long that they had little use for the yellowish stuff now offered them. Only time and education made a place for unbleached flour on the tables of Rochdale consumers.

For three years the mill produced excellent flour and husky financial losses—losses which frightened the faint-hearted and set the tongues of calamity prophets to wagging. Capital began to be withdrawn from the society; members threatened to withdraw. But, at last, with the help of other groups who were copying their methods a market for the surplus was found and the mill became a paying proposition.

Reserves, wisely set aside during the first years of operation of the store, were sufficient to absorb the losses on this first experiment in manufacturing. The storm blew over and was forgotten. Years brought increasing confidence in the whole enterprise. Faith, business volume, capital investment, and membership in the society grew together.

The organization of the Rochdale Pioneers was the beginning of Consumers Co-operation, a development which slowly envelops the world. The movement is active in practically every country on the globe. Wherever it is found it is creating a new class of property owners. Its membership today is not known exactly but it is pretty safe to say that not less than 65,000,000 families are identified with it.

The Rochdale society was not England's first co-operative. It was not even the first to attempt the operation of a store. Between the years 1828 and 1832 there arose in Great Britain what is known as the Union Shop movement. Its guiding spirit was a London physician named William King. Dr. King ministered to working-class families. He saw their suffering and their frequent illnesses—caused so largely by their poverty. He became deeply concerned about the conditions which the industrial revolution had created and, like Owen, wanted to do something about them. He was a disciple of the first great prophet of modern times but not subservient to his thinking. He attached greater importance to consumer action. Perhaps his experience as a physician made him much more conscious of the need for better food and clothing in poor families than was Owen, the successful *producer*. Perhaps he saw in the operation of something as simple as a store, a technique that was within the range of the ability of English laborers. Anyway, he did encourage the co-operative ownership of stores by consumers as a means by which the poor could do something toward helping themselves.

By 1830 there were one hundred and seventy Union Shops scattered over England. A Union Shop was a society of workers organized as consumers. By 1832 the number had grown to four hundred. Dr. King published a magazine called *The Co-operator* in which he encouraged these organizations and tried his best to guide them to success. Many thoughtful people felt that the Union Shops were destined to play an important role in the future of the nation's poorer people. But the next two years shattered their dreams. One by one the stores began to collapse. By 1835 only here and there among the Scotch and North Englanders were Union Shops to be found. The rest had failed. The few that did survive were forgotten and rediscovered by a later generation, made *store*-conscious by the Rochdale success.

There were several causes which contributed to the collapse of the Union Shops. Those causes can be summed up in a single word—inexperience. Store-keeping had for generations been wholly a matter of private enterprise. No one knew how to make it a social undertaking. King, and the other intellectuals who assisted in giving the movement leadership, were as completely in the dark about organizational techniques as those whom they attempted to help.

Some of the Union Shops failed because they did a credit business; some because they became involved in price wars with richer and wiser competitors. Not a few were destroyed by inner strife brought on by efforts to control the religion, morals, and politics of members. Some were robbed by directors and managers who stole their funds—taking advantage of the fact that these organizations had no legal standing and hence no protection under the law. Some were destroyed by their very prosperity. They made money but had no acceptable way of distributing the funds created. A part paid dividends on shares as did the ordinary business firm. The primary interest of shareholders came to center on dividends and all co-operative features were forgotten. Other groups used their profits to set up manufacturing enterprises in which members were given employment. In these, jealousy arose between those who were given work and those who wanted it. A number of the Union Shops had permitted men to vote according to the number of shares they held. If they were prosperous the larger shareholders eventually gained control and operated the business for their own personal advantage.

The Rochdale Pioneers succeeded because of their canny ability to profit by the mistakes of others. They knew the Union Shop movement and had the intelligence to learn from its failures.

They refused to be political, religious, or moral partisans. If they had insisted on allegiance to any political or religious creed as a qualification for membership they would have had the merriest kind of dog fight in the very beginning. Among the original twenty-eight were Owenites, Christian Socialists, Chartists, and even ardent temperance advocates. Toleration was essential to the very life of their organization. They practiced the principle of religious and political neutrality from the very beginning. It remained their practice through the passing years.

In order to avoid price wars they decided to charge the current market prices on the goods they sold. They avoided the pitfalls of a credit business by insisting on cash trading. In order that members might be kept accurately informed as to the affairs of the business they insisted on frequent and regular audits of the books.

Control was placed in the hands of a board of directors, democratically elected by the membership. Each member was allowed but one vote in all elections and only those who would take the trouble to attend meetings were allowed the franchise. Proxy voting was not permitted.

They believed that those who created the capital for the operation of their business should have some reward for so doing. That reward they set at five per cent interest, which was the current rate.

What to do with earnings above five per cent on capital was a tough problem. The mistakes of the Union Shops were very fresh in their memory. And yet to find a detour around them was not easy. There were no precedents to guide them. Something new was necessary. Originality is rare indeed. Long hours of discussion simply took them back over familiar paths. Finally one of their number had a happy thought: why not give back the earnings to the patrons of the business on the basis of their patronage? After all the patrons created the earnings. Each patron contributed to them in exact proportion to the amount he purchased through the society. The problem was solved. This simple scheme was adopted. It was freighted with great wisdom.

This method of distributing earnings was the one original thing in the Rochdale formula. Their other practices had precedents in the varied experiments of the Union Shop movement. It is extremely doubtful if any other method would have worked. It had the double virtue of being thoroughly just and of giving those who supported the store, a tangible in-hand reward for faithful support. The patronage refund is rooted in human realism. It appeals at once to man's sense of fairness and to his self-interest.

Also the Pioneers had the foresight to see that an intelligent membership is essential to the proper functioning of democratic group effort. Though most of them were illiterate, they had no boorish disrespect for knowledge. Rather they were determined to equip themselves intellectually for the role which they hoped to play in changing the status of the exploited laborer. Accordingly, they determined from the very beginning that their co-operative society should also be an educational institution. They used some of the earnings of the business for the maintenance of a library and a reading room. They constantly sought to make themselves and others intelligent about their business, general economics, and the social order in which they lived.

The Rochdale practices have long since been worked into a simple code of behavior for consumers' co-operative societies. The laws of this code are usually given as follows:

First, there are three rules called the *Fundamental Principles of Consumers' Co-operation.*

(1.) Democratic control. That means one vote per member without regard to the number of shares held. Owning one share or ten makes no difference in control. Members vote as persons, and not as owners of a given portion of the capital.

(2.) Returns to capital shall not be more than

the minimum prevailing rate of interest. Dividends do not go skyrocketing with earnings. The Pioneers set the interest rate at five per cent but the percentage is left to the discretion of the members of each society. This principle eliminates speculation. Co-operative shares do not fluctuate in value with earnings.

(3.) After operating expenses are paid, reserves and education cared for, interest paid, the remainder of earnings are distributed to patrons on the basis of patronage. The one who spends the most with a society gets the most in return.

With these principles go certain methods which are sometimes called the *Methods of Consumers' Co-operation;* sometimes the *Secondary Principles of Consumers' Co-operation.*

(1.) Open membership. No one shall be denied membership in a co-operative society unless it is known he wishes to join for the purpose of making trouble for the organization.

(2.) Political and religious neutrality. Members shall be left free to support any or no political or religious sect as conscience dictates.

(3.) Non-members may buy their way into membership. They may do it by purchasing a share of stock or by simply giving their trade to the organization. Non-members often receive their portion of the patrons' refund in terms of credit toward their initial shares. As soon as the refund equals the value of a share of stock the patron automatically becomes a member with full voting privileges.

(4.) A portion of the earnings shall be spent for the education of members and non-members. Usually, though not always, education is confined to spreading knowledge of the techniques, philosophy, and history of co-operation.

(5.) Labor shall be fairly treated. Every effort is put forth to make working conditions as ideal as circumstances will permit.

(6.) Business shall be done for cash.

(7.) Current market prices shall be charged.

(8.) Adequate reserves for depreciation, expansion, and unforeseen difficulties shall be regularly set aside.

(9.) Where possible, co-operative societies shall combine their strength in democratic associations for the purposes of wholesaling, manufacturing, and providing services too large to be undertaken by local organizations.

These things combined with intelligent management were responsible for the success of the Rochdale Pioneers. Experience has proven the soundness of their building. Where these principles have been violated failure has resulted. Where they have been adhered to, other groups have been able to achieve similar successes.

Between the years 1879 and 1889 eight hundred forty-four co-operative societies failed in England.

Those failures were largely the result of violation of some part of the above code. Similar failures elsewhere have largely been due to the same cause. In the hard school of experience men have learned the necessity of strict adherence to Rochdale practice. It is essential to success.

CHAPTER IV

Progress

NOTHING SUCCEEDS LIKE SUCCESS. As soon as the Pioneers had demonstrated that co-operatively owned stores were a practical possibility, the distressed workers of other communities began to organize societies. During 1847 and 1848 stores were started in a number of nearby towns: Bacup, Todmorden, Leigh, Salford, Padiham, and Middletown. These were all in north England not far from the Scottish border. Perhaps it took the English ability to muddle through, influenced by the thrift of the Scotch, to make a success of the plodding idea that organizing co-operative stores had something to do with changing the status of those who earn their bread by the sweat of their brow.

By 1852 there were one hundred and thirty societies in north England and the Scottish Midlands. Some of these operated on the Rochdale plan; some did not. Some were the isolated survivors of the Union Shop debacle. They were all small. Their average membership was fifty. Rochdale stood head and shoulders above the rest with its six hundred. By 1860 all were operating on the Rochdale plan.

Three years later the total number of societies was four hundred twenty-six.

The years since 1850 had witnessed a growing sense of common purpose among them. In '63 the first steps were taken toward setting up a commercial federation for furthering mutual ends. The Rochdale society took the lead in calling together representatives of the various local groups for the discussion of common problems. From that time onwards such conferences were a regular feature of the co-operative calendar. The sense of unity ripened into the conviction that co-operation between co-operatives might have in it greater possibilities than just the exchange of ideas. A buying federation was the logical next move.

The steps by which this idea took form cannot be accurately traced. As early as 1859 William Cooper of Rochdale suggested that the Pioneers might undertake to act as a wholesaling agent for some of the nearby smaller societies. A small group of experienced store founders considered the idea of a co-operative wholesale in 1860. That year witnessed the establishment of a little news sheet called *The Co-operator* which advocated the establishment of such a central organization.

At a meeting held on Good Friday in 1863 the representatives of some of the leading organizations committed themselves to the creation of "The North of England Co-operative Wholesale Agency and

Depot Society, Limited." By the close of the year the wholesale society—burdened with its sonorous name —had been organized. Business operation began in 1864.

Five years of thinking, planning, and hard work were behind the formation of the wholesale but its first years did not altogether justify the roseate dreams of its founders. It was the creation of men whose vision encompassed the coming years. Not all members of local societies were interested in the future. Most of them were much more concerned with the immediate task of keeping their retail enterprises on an even keel. Store managers, who had gotten used to bargaining with private wholesales and had developed pride in their ability to haggle in the general market, did not feel very great enthusiasm for giving the bulk of their trade to this new organization. The first report and balance sheet of the wholesale showed that only fifty-four societies had become shareholders in it and but thirty-two of those had bothered to send delegates to the semi-annual meeting.

But though the existing provincialism and backwardness of societies and managers slowed up growth, it did not check it. 1866 saw the turnover of the wholesale pass the million dollar mark. The success of that year's business was the turning point. The next year business jumped fifty per cent and saw two hundred and fifty societies in active support of it.

Then came home building. At a cost of $20,000 a six-story headquarters building was erected at the corner of Balloon Street and Garden in Manchester. Early in 1869 it was dedicated with fitting ceremonies.

It was a modest step forward in the quiet assumption of property ownership by people of small means —whose sole economic power lay in the shillings they traded across the counters of retail stores.

In 1868 the Scotch followed in the footsteps of their English cousins. They founded a wholesale society at Glasgow.

In the meantime the societies of northeast England were complaining about the distance from Manchester to the river Tyne. They wanted wholesaling service nearer home. They persuaded the wholesale's board of directors to establish a branch at Newcastle. They promised faithful and loyal support, and gave it. The branch opened with three employees in May, 1872. The first year's business topped $750,000. On January 2, 1874, a $65,000 home for the Newcastle offices and warehouses was opened.

By that year the number of co-operative stores in England had grown to nearly nine hundred. The aggregate membership was three hundred thousand families; the invested capital $15,000,000; the annual sales $50,000,000; net earnings $4,500,000. Scotland had two hundred stores, fifty thousand members; sales totaled $7,500,000; net earnings were $700,000; the capital invested $1,250,000.

Manufacturing was the next step. The first products were biscuits and sweets. A factory was purchased by the wholesale in 1873. Headaches for the management and losses were the first results of this venture. The machinery of the factory was antiquated and had to be modernized. Experienced management was hard to find. It took three years to get the venture on a paying basis but at last the Crumpsall Biscuit works became a satisfactory part of the co-operative empire. Boot and shoe manufacturing got under way in a rented factory the same year the biscuit factory was purchased. This worked out very well from the start. The plant was purchased in 1874 and enlarged a year later. A committee report given in December 1876 boasts of producing 8,000 pairs of shoes a week with an employee group of over four hundred. Soap manufacturing started in 1874.

Thirty years after the opening of the Toad Lane store at Rochdale saw the co-operators well launched into the field of production. Another part of the Pioneers' program had become a reality. It had not come quite as they visualized it. Manufacturing had not been undertaken primarily to provide employment for unemployed co-operators. The plants were not owned by the Rochdale society alone. These factories were started for the purpose of making goods for consumers; they were owned by the co-operative wholesale society which was in turn owned by the eight hundred local co-operatives scattered across England. A third of a million families were represented in those local groups. The combined resources of those families did make it possible for them to join the ranks of owners of business and industry. They were building themselves an economic empire.

Another conquest came in 1876. The sea has a peculiar significance for the Britisher. Ruling the waves is an old custom with the people of Great Britain. Co-operators decided to share in that rule. They had reason to complain of the treatment given them by shipping companies so they bought the S.S. *Plover*, a little vessel of 250 tons. They found that ruling the waves secured for them many favors. The railroads lowered freight rates; continental merchants gave better prices. The *Plover* greeted a sister ship in 1879—the S.S. *Pioneer* of 650 tons. The *Cambrian* was added to the fleet in 1881.

The private shipping interests were greatly irritated by this invasion of their economic realm. A price war was declared. The co-operative wholesale decided to fight it out. A fourth ship was purchased. Shipping magnates openly expressed their contempt toward "working men butting in on something they knew nothing about." This but steeled the resolve of the co-operators to see the scrap through.

They cheerfully wrote off their losses until the "interests" sued for peace. An economic war had been waged and won. Vessel after vessel was added with the passing of time until a fleet of eleven ships carried goods for the co-operatives. Most of the boats were sold early in the present century because of changed conditions in the shipping trade. But the disinherited commoners had had a taste of ship-owning and they liked it.

It is interesting to note that in 1894, when Manchester was made a seaport by the completion of an expensive shipping canal to the ocean, the S.S. *Pioneer* was the first vessel to dock at the pier. The first cargo landed in Manchester, the seaport, was sugar from Rouen—imported for the tables of the *working class*. When the *Pioneer* was lashed to the dock, the Mayor of Salford was among those who stepped aboard to extend congratulations to the captain.

That incident is a symbol of the growing favor which co-operators enjoyed in the eyes of politicians. The Rochdale society had begun business in 1844 under the Friendly Societies Act of 1836. That act declared that such societies should do business only with members. The co-operators disregarded the provision. Their practice was made legal in 1852 by the passage of the Industrial and Provident Acts. In 1862 the bill was further amended at the request of co-operators in order to make legal the proposed wholesale. Its amendment was materially aided by the reading of co-operative records in Parliament. The law makers were signally impressed with the cold facts and figures of business success. These acts were revised again in 1876 when the wholesale wanted to open a banking department. Those who own property are listened to in the halls of government.

Banking as a co-operative enterprise was first undertaken seriously in 1872. In that year a group of the northern societies organized an independent bank. Four years later it failed through mismanagement. Following the revision of co-operative law in the year of this failure the wholesale set up a banking department of its own. This second venture, begun with some misgivings, was successful from the very start. Co-operatives the country over used it as a depository for funds. Individual co-operators carried accounts with it. Credit was made available to societies needing it. The entire movement found the new bank a great source of economic strength.

Flour milling was one of the first manufacturing processes undertaken by co-operative societies. Attention has already been called to the first Rochdale venture in this field. Other societies likewise went into it. Some of the larger ones owned mills individually. In other cases federations of small groups were created and the mills were owned by the federations. By 1880 there were between thirty and forty of these small co-operatively owned mills. Until that time the wholesale, out of respect for local enterprises, had kept out of the milling field. But gradually it became apparent that flour milling was becoming a big business. Profit-making corporations were erecting plants capable of turning out hundreds of sacks a day. The small mills were not able to compete with these industrial Goliaths. Only one co-operative organization was big enough to undertake milling on the scale which the new conditions demanded. That was the wholesale. In 1886 the representatives of local societies, assembled in annual meeting, passed a resolution empowering the directors to build a plant.

They moved slowly at first, realizing the importance of a good location with needed rail and water transportation. They finally chose a site near Dunston on the Tyne. It was purchased and work started preparing the ground for the erection of the mill. In 1889 the need for it became suddenly urgent. Private manufacturers had set afoot plans for the creation of a national flour trust which would include all the large mills from Humber to the Tweed. The co-operators did not propose to be at the tender mercies of any such combination. They pushed their own project with renewed energy and at a cost of $600,000 built a plant having a capacity of forty sacks per hour. It was formally opened April 18, 1891, with great jubilation.

In spite of its elaborate birthday party it proceeded forthwith to lose money for its owners. At the end of four years the losses totaled $150,000. This was not altogether the fault of the management. The wheat market of the world had gone chaotic and there was no controlling it. When the market finally settled down the mill began to make money and continued to do so for long years.

Large as was the Dunston mill it was all too small to meet the co-operative market for flour. The wholesale continued to import great quantities of this household necessity. A second and larger plant was ready for work in 1900. No celebration was held when its wheels started turning. The deficits piled up by the first venture were too fresh in the memory. The third and fourth mills came in 1902 and 1910. When the wholesale—whose name had in the meantime been shortened to Co-operative Wholesale Society and popularly abbreviated to C.W.S.—celebrated its Golden Jubilee in 1913, the mills which it owned were turning out two hundred fifty sacks of flour each hour of the day and night.

Through the succeeding years the C.W.S. has steadily expanded. It is today the largest single food distributing business in the world. Its flour mills are the largest and most modern in the Empire; its textile factories hold a like position. It owns nearly one hundred and fifty manufacturing enterprises. These turn out not only food and clothing but automobiles and radios as well. Its properties include 30,000 acres of tea plantations in India and Ceylon, olive farms in Africa, acres and acres of farm land in England, producing food and drink for the 8,000,000 families which are now a part of the English consumers' co-operative movement. The banking department is fourth in financial strength to the Bank of England. The general insurance department, established in 1898, is writing one-half the insurance of the nation.

This steady growth of the wholesale must be thought of as a result. The cause was the steady expansion of local consumers' societies. It buys only for them, manufactures only for their needs. The central organization is their property and dedicated to their service. Across the counters of the retail stores moves an eighth of England's retail business. To an ever increasing degree the local societies are providing members with all the goods and service important for good human living. The movement started in a grocery store. It did not end there. The services which it provides now include food, clothing, furniture, automobiles, medicine, home construction, furniture, jewelry, fuel, drugs, credit, insurance, and even undertaking. In a slow, plodding fashion the consumers have been expanding their control over the means of production and distribution.

CHAPTER V

The Learned Can Be Wrong

THE LAST TWO CHAPTERS have been misleading. They have given the impression that the consumers' co-operative movement had a steady and unchecked growth—unattended by the usual problems and controversies which go along with the ordinary development of human institutions. Such certainly was not the case. During the first half-century it grew when even some of its friends questioned its right to a place in the sun. The movement owes a debt of gratitude to Robert Owen for effectively proclaiming the necessity of social control of machines. But it took fifty years for it to recover from Owen.

He glorified man's role as a producer. He sincerely hoped for the day when workers in factories would own them. It was inevitable that he should think in those terms. Back of him lay the centuries of hand production in which the men who produced owned their own tools. The shoemaker had been owner of his awl and last, the weaver his loom, the spinner his wheel, the smith his forge and anvil. Machine production made these hand tools relics. Those who worked with them became laborers in factories which other men owned. Owen wanted to restore the possession of the tools of production to those who were the producers. He saw that collective ownership of machines was necessary to this end. He wanted to substitute collective ownership of machines for the former private ownership of hand tools. This, for him, was the way to restore labor to its former dignity.

He attached some value to having the workers own their own stores but he had no large sympathy with grocery store co-operation. It was a good method of making a meager income go further—nothing more. It was just a penny-saving device. Producers' co-operation was the pure form. All other forms of collective enterprise were subordinate to it.

Most of the immediate followers of Owen shared his point of view. The Rochdale Pioneers probably accepted his general idea. There is evidence that they started with a store because they realized that it was all their meager resources made possible. They may have felt that the store would create savings sufficient to establish a producers' organization. The haste with which they rushed into the purchase of a flour mill with a producing capacity far beyond their immediate needs indicated their basic producer interest. It is, of course, impossible to determine accurately their motives and purposes. Their meager records—mostly minutes of their meetings—leave much to conjecture. It is difficult indeed to read the events of the past with the mind of the past.

The mantle of Robert Owen fell at his death upon a group known as the Christian Socialists. They were churchmen who shared his concern over the state of the nation but who did not share his antagonism to Christianity. Charles Kingsley and Thomas Hughes were the best known of their number. All were men of education and ability.

They were thoroughly enamored with Owen's idea about worker ownership. They, like him, preached it in season and out. Laborers should own the machines they tended and use the profits of production for mutual benefit. One of them states their point of view in these words: "Theoretically the idea we endeavored to spread was the conception of workers as brethren—of work as coming from a brotherhood of men associated for their common benefit—who therefore rejected any notion of competition with each other as inconsistent with the true form of society. And without formally preaching communism, we sought to form industrial establishments communistic in feeling, of which it should be the aim, while paying ordinary wages and interest ... to apply the profits of the business in ways conducive to the common advantage of the body of those *whose work produced them.*"

When the magazine *The Co-operator* appeared in 1860 the Christian Socialists dominated its editorial policies. When the Co-operative Union was formed —a federation of societies organized for spreading co-operative propaganda and for fighting the legislative battles of the movement—the Christian Socialists were prominent in it. One of their number, Vansittart Neale, was its executive secretary for many years.

It is interesting to note that the intellectual leaders of the Union, whose membership was largely made up of consumers' societies, were for half a century men whose primary interest was in promoting another type of economic action.

Owen and his Christian disciples had an excellent idea. There was only one thing wrong with it: it wouldn't work. These men organized many societies of producers. They invested capital in them; lauded them as being the highest form of co-operation. But such societies had a most disagreeable habit of failing. All the idealism of the Christian Socialists could not keep such enterprises on an even keel. Workers' co-operatives simply refused to stay solvent.

Faith has a strange habit of persisting in spite of evidence. These men were not at all discouraged by the failure of one after another of their pet schemes. They were constantly at work promoting new ones to replace those that expired.

The directors of the co-operative wholesale were, during the early years, completely dominated by Christian Socialist ideas. As a result the wholesale subscribed time after time to stock in producers' organizations. Not a single voice was raised in protest against such appropriations. The co-operators were all orthodox Owenites.

They did not all remain so, however. Deficits are hard to argue with. As the directors saw wholesale funds lost time after time, skepticism began to develop. Enthusiasm for investment in producers' co-operatives began to wane. As enthusiasm cooled, hot arguments appeared in the co-operative press. The board rooms of store societies rang with heated discussions.

Further fat was added to the flames when the C.W.S. started production on its own account. The Christian Socialists were very suspicious of this process. The organized consumers were invading a field which ought to be kept sacred for "pure" types of co-operatives. For the wholesale to take such action was in their eyes treason to the fundamental purposes of co-operation.

When it became apparent that the wholesale would persist in its heresy, schemes for having the workers share in profits and in management were brought forward. The wholesale directors tried and rejected them because they failed to work in practice. A divided managerial responsibility was simply impractical. With the abandonment of these schemes came louder protests from sincere men who believed that man, the worker, was more important than man, the consumer.

In 1874 there came to the presidency of the

wholesale a quiet man by the name of John T. W. Mitchell. He was the first to challenge seriously the dominant Owenite philosophy of some of his associates. He lacked all the advantages of formal education which some of his antagonists had enjoyed. He was born of obscure parentage in the back of a saloon. He received most of his schooling in a Congregational Sunday School of Rochdale. But he had native wit and the intelligence to grasp the basic facts of a situation. Co-operation was a passion with him —but a passion disciplined by a mind that refused to ignore results and the stubborn testimony of balance sheets. He defended the moral right of consumers to control their own affairs. He stood at the fore in many heated debates in congresses of the Co-operative Union and in conferences of C.W.S. directors.

The Christian Socialists, with the eloquence and the studied phrases of school-trained men, spoke of the sacred rights of labor. Mitchell took his stand on an ancient platform of Adam Smith, "Consumption is the sole end of all production: and the interest of the producer ought to be attended to only so far as it may be necessary for promoting that of the consumer." He insisted that consumers were the whole public, while workers were only a portion of the public. The interest of the whole ought to be set above the interest of a part.

Mitchell and his opponents were alike perfectly

sincere in their contentions but events fought the battle for him. The consumers' movement grew and got things done. The producers' associations consistently failed. Finally, when Mitchell was within three years of the end of an eventful, useful life, a new champion arose to defend his point of view—a woman, Beatrice Potter, who later became Mrs. Sidney Webb. In 1891 she published a book, *The Co-operative Movement in Great Britain,* which was simply a marshaling of the evidence. She laid to public view the record of the two types of organization: producers and consumers. Facts triumphed over the eloquence and persistent faith of the Christian Socialists. The dominant idea of Owen had run its course so far as the co-operative movement of Great Britain was concerned.

His basic conception was tried in the crucible of experience and found wanting. The co-operative store which he held to be of minor significance to the desires of the meek to become property owners proved itself to be all important.

With that controversy settled the co-operative movement became self-conscious. It had come to know its own power and to see its own purpose. Maturity replaced the strain and stress of adolescence. Time and energy, which had been spent in endless debate and in chasing after the unattainable, was now harnessed to an expanding program of economic conquest. Co-operation moved forward to its present place in the economic life of England. The nation whose inventors ushered mankind into a new economic era gave the world a business technique by which machines can be harnessed to the task of satisfying human hungers.

CHAPTER VI

Around the World

CONSUMERS' CO-OPERATION arose amid the social unrest which followed the wars of Napoleon. It was the child of the Industrial Revolution. It was the result of a search for a pattern of business organization which would properly distribute the riches machine production helped create. It came first in England because the Industrial Revolution began there.

However, it is not an English movement. As the modern techniques of production spread around the world the economic problems which it created spread with it. Out of the efforts to solve them came like results—consumers' co-operatives followed the spinning jenny, the power loom, the steam engine, when they went globe trotting. Scotland established her first Rochdale co-operative society in 1851. Denmark and Russia followed fifteen years later. Sweden tried in the sixties but couldn't make the idea work until the present century. Finland had a like experience. France had successful stores as early as 1885.

Iceland, Switzerland, Belgium, Hungary, Jugoslavia, Norway, Holland, Estonia, Lithuania, Bulgaria, Italy, Greece, Poland, Rumania, Spain,

Portugal, Argentina, Mexico, Australia, New Zealand, India, Japan, China, Palestine, Canada, South Africa, Turkey, Armenia, Egypt, and the United States all have important co-operative movements.

Some of these countries have made economic history. The story of Sweden's conquest of recurring depressions, of Finland's growing peace and security for the masses of her people has become good news in a world of gloom. Denmark has written a saga of heroic economic and cultural achievement. Hers is the tale of a small nation, defeated in war, with meager natural resources, rising to social greatness in a generation. In thirty-five years she revolutionized her business life, reduced farm tenancy from fifty per cent to five, and has made security and culture available to all her people.

Iceland is the most completely co-operative country in the world and she has the smallest percentage of illiteracy of any nation on the globe. In Belgium the movement has been an important factor in making it possible for her to support Europe's greatest density of population. The Swiss have used co-operation as a technique for making good living possible in a mountainous region. The common people of Russia have managed to build a powerful movement in spite of the opposition of the Tsars, war, revolution, and the excesses of her state socialism. Even saber-rattling Mussolini has bowed to

economic realities and permitted the Italians to co-
operate as consumers to provide themselves with
food, shelter, and clothing.

Germany alone of the world's major countries
has a prostrate movement. Naziism has thus far
been definitely anti-co-operative in ideology and action. Only vestiges remain of her once powerful co-
operatives. Time and time alone will tell as to
whether studied hostility is a passing or permanent
policy of the Third Reich.

All the countries mentioned have co-operative
wholesales. Many have seen the consumers going
far in manufacturing things for themselves.

The co-operators of the world are united in an
international, interracial fellowship called the International Co-operative Alliance.

The idea of some such organization was germane
with Robert Owen. In 1835 he founded an Association of All Classes of All Nations. By 1836 it
had two hundred seven members—all residents of
London. Owen defined the objective of the organization in the following terms: "The object of the
association is to effect peaceably and by reason alone
an entire change in the character and condition of
mankind, by establishing over the world the principle
and practice of the religion of charity for the con-
victions, feelings, and conduct of all individuals,
without distinction of sex, class, sect, party, country,
or color *combined with a well devised equitable and*

natural system of united property . . . for producing and distributing in the best manner the best qualities of all kinds of wealth abundantly for all."

In 1837 he made a trip to Paris, Munich, and Vienna to interest others in his idea. But Owen's dream was a spirit without a body. By 1879, however, a sense of international co-operative fellowship had begun to grow. When the national congress of British societies was held at Whitsuntide, eighteen persons from other countries were present. The number included Dr. Edward Pfeiffer and Victor Aime Huber, co-operative pioneers of Germany; Professor Vigano, who initiated co-operation in Italy; Rev. H. Christian Sonne, father of the Danish development; Axel Krook, who tried in vain to interest the Swedes in the idea; and representatives from Switzerland and Greece.

Further developments came in 1885. By that time the number of societies in France had become sufficiently large to make desirable the formation of a national federation. E. de Boyne was one of the guiding spirits in the French development. He had organized a successful local society at Nîmes. He nurtured the idea of forming the French Co-operative Union. When that organization was being born, he invited representatives of the English societies to come as fraternal delegates and give counsel and encouragement. This invitation was gladly accepted. The next year, 1886, de Boyne went to the English congress and there proposed that an international union of co-operatives be formed.

The proposal bore no immediate fruit. For one thing de Boyne himself had no clear idea of the function of such an organization. In the address presenting the matter he talked vaguely about the need for an international organization to arbitrate the disputes between employers and employees which were making the industrial world a great battle-ground.

The International Alliance finally did get under way in 1895. The first congress was held in London beginning August 19. Earl Gray was the first chairman of this consumers' league of nations. French, Belgian, Dutch, Swiss, and Danish societies sent delegates. One American, L. O. Nelson, was present and was made a member of the provisional central committee.

The first years of the Alliance were marked by controversy. The fight between the Christian Socialists and John T. W. Mitchell in England was reflected in the international organization. In fact, the Christian Socialists took a leading part in creating the Alliance for the very purpose of using it as an instrument for furthering their ideas. It was their last battle line in the hopeless defense of producers' co-operation as the one right and exalted form of mutual aid. They asserted that only those business enterprises which shared earnings and management with the laborers were true co-operatives and altogether righteous. In their opinion private businesses which maintained schemes of profit-sharing with labor were more to be desired than consumer-owned enterprises that did not.

In accordance with this fixed and unshakable idea they sent out a call in 1892 to both co-operatives and interested individuals asking for an Alliance that would support the profit-sharing scheme: "We propose that the alliance of which we invite formation, shall not be confined to co-operative societies or their members, but shall include all firms or companies which accept the principle of the participation of the worker in profit as part of their constitution or systematic practice, and all persons, whether heads of industrial bodies or not, who signify their approval of this principle by becoming members of the alliance."

This proposal was toned down by 1895, but its basic idea was foremost in the minds of many who attended the first congress. In fact, the chairman, Earl Gray, declared in his opening address, "The question which will occupy our chief attention during this week is the consideration of how we can best promote in industrial enterprises the profit-sharing principle."

The fight over profit-sharing was not alone responsible for making the early years of the Alliance a period of strain and stress. Its loose membership requirements aggravated matters. All kinds of organizations were admitted; consumers' societies, agricultural marketing associations, producers' co-operatives, and even profit-sharing private businesses. This made for a lack of common purpose and common philosophy. Individuals were allowed to become members on payment of a contribution to the budget. This brought in a lunatic fringe—men with pet ideas, who by joining the Alliance could buy an audience which they could obtain in no other way. Much of the talking in early congresses was done by the latter group.

Gradually, however, the growing power of the consumers' societies made itself felt. The individual memberships were abolished and voting placed on a delegate representative basis. The continued failure of worker-owned co-operative production societies in England slowly silenced the advocates of profit-sharing. Leaders of consumers' co-operatives were perfecting a philosophy which gave moral justification for a procedure which had shown itself to be sound in practice.

Matters came to a head in 1904 at the congress of the Alliance held in Budapest. Hans Müller of the Swiss Co-operative Union closed an address on "The Organization of Consumers' Societies in Rural and Semi-rural Districts" with these words: "Co-operation is an economic and social movement for liberty, which, by means of the organized building

up of a new order of the economic and social conditions on which our existence depends, aims at ob-
taining both for the individual and the people at
large, a great amount of independence. Therefore,
whoever sincerely desires to promote the co-operative movement in any respect whatever must never
forget to banish the old state of dependency and to
be most careful never to replace it by any similar
institution."

A debate followed in which Dr. Müller asserted
his firm belief that the end and goal of co-operation
was the abolition of the dependence of the common
people upon the institutions of capitalism for the
goods necessary for abundant human living. Its de-
sign and purpose was the building of a new social
order in which the exploitation and inefficiencies of
capitalism were no more.

Conservatives were alarmed by such sentiments,
but the Congress, as a whole, saw in Dr. Müller's
statement only a logical and clear-cut presentation
of the basic purpose of the movement.

Not only did this congress declare it the purpose
of co-operatives to free the consumers from their
dependence on capitalism; it also asserted that co-
opcratives should keep themselves free from dependence upon the state: asking and accepting no
subsidies or loans from government. Representatives
of agricultural marketing associations were offended

at this, for they loved to have their organizations sustained by public funds.

The total result was the loss of some members. The marketing association dropped out of the picture as did some of the more conservative consumers' groups—particularly the German. But the next few years saw the ranks filled with new organizations having the philosophy of such leaders as Hans Müller. Unity of purpose replaced the divisions of the first years. Definiteness and decision took hold of the Alliance. It had achieved maturity. From 1904 on it has been a consumers' Internationale dedicated to giving the common man better access to food, shelter, and clothing.

Today forty countries are represented in the membership of the International Co-operative Alliance. Over 193,000 local societies having more than 65,000,000 shareholding members are included in its great fellowship.

The Alliance is a people's league of nations. It is not controlled by diplomats representing imperialistic and warring governments but by those who see in collective activity as consumers a means of achieving a better human society. Instead of plotting and counter-plotting in contests for position and power, the delegates at its congresses plan ways and means for making mutual aid more effective in economic processes. The needs of the common man are the same the world over. The basic hungers for food and clothing, for adequate shelter, and some of the beauties and luxuries which make civilized living possible, are present in every race and nationality.

When it began, the Alliance was primarily a fellowship of like-minded people who met for the purpose of swapping ideas and experiences. But now the tie of common ownership of the means of production and distribution is giving torso and limbs to its spirit of brotherhood. International co-operative wholesaling has become a reality.

The English and Scottish Wholesales own their tea plantations in India and Ceylon together. Danes, Finlanders, Swedes, and Norwegians are served by an international wholesale society with headquarters at Copenhagen. This organization is binding the consumers of all four countries into a closer and closer unity. The successful "Luma" electric light bulb factory is their common property.

The Alliance has assisted in the creation of an International Co-operative Wholesale Society which is actively engaged in promoting trade between the co-operatives of various countries. It began operations in 1924. The volume of its business steadily increases. It is now more than $20,000,000 per annum. Committees are at work preparing for an international co-operative bank and an international insurance society.

CHAPTER VII

In Nineteenth Century America

THE FACTORY SYSTEM which so seriously disturbed the social and business life of England came to America very soon after it had gotten under way in the mother country. In 1789 a mechanic named Samuel Slater came to the New World bringing with him a first hand knowledge of the production methods developed by Hargreaves, Arkwright, and Watt. He bore neither blueprints nor drawings, for it was a criminal offense for anyone to carry out of England sketches or models of machinery. He carried his plans and models in his head.

He built the first American mill at Pawtucket, Rhode Island, completing it on December 21, 1790. Sixteen years later he and a brother constructed large factories near Slaterville in the same state. By 1810 the United States had over one hundred manufacturing plants in operation, all of them erected according to Slater models.

Thus machine production was smuggled into America.

Its arrival brought suffering to American labor as it had to the English working men. Long hours, low wages, child labor became the rule. The writings

of Seth Luther and James Montgomery, first American students of labor problems, bear witness. They report that working days were from twelve to fifteen hours in length; wages sixty-five to seventy cents. Sometimes the lash was used to stimulate production; not infrequently deductions were made from wages to support churches which pious employers required their employees to attend. In 1831 fifty-eight per cent of the factory workers of the industrial East were women and seven per cent children under twelve years of age.

Against such conditions men revolted. A few intellectuals became apostles of Robert Owen. He came to America in 1824 to preach his doctrines and establish a co-operative village at New Harmony, Indiana. His preachments moved some of the finest spirits in America to take up the battle for better conditions. Horace Mann began his great fight for free education. The Rev. George Ripley established the famous Brook Farm Colony in 1841 which was an attempt to show the way to Utopia. The followers of Charles Fourier dotted the country with Phalanxes—operating on the principles of Owen's co-operative villages and failing as consistently.

The working people themselves created trade unions and political parties to fight for a ten-hour day and better wages. Strikes were by no means infrequent. Most of this agitation got nowhere against

an indifferent public opinion. The population of America was predominantly rural and the farmers saw no sense in the demand for a ten-hour day. Clergymen preached against it on the grounds that men should be contented with their wages and on behalf of the glory of work and the dangers of idleness. Manufacturers opposed it for obvious reasons.

One of the numerous labor organizations born previous to the American Civil War was the New England Workingmen's Association, organized in Brahmin Boston in 1844. It was this group which first saw the possibilities of laborers bettering themselves by working together as consumers.

Shortly after its organization John Kaulback, a tailor, brought forward the suggestion that interest and attendance at meetings would be stimulated if the members formed a buying club, raised a little capital, and bought household necessities together. This was done. Substantial savings were made over regular store prices.

The membership soon became so engrossed in the co-operative buying program that it overshadowed all other purposes of the Association. In 1845 a store was established as a means "of bettering the condition of the working class."

The management was instructed to sell at prices which would defray the actual costs of operations and pay a maximum of six per cent on invested capital. Business was to be done for cash. Persons not of

"good moral character" or users of intoxicants were not permitted to own shares.

The move seemed timely. The store flourished. By 1847 twelve groups of people were operating businesses on these principles. They banded themselves together in what was called the Workingmen's Protective Union. Two years later the name was changed to New England Protective Union. By 1850, 106 local Unions were operating stores. The 83 whose records are known reported a combined capital of $72,000, a membership of 5,100, and sales totaling $650,000. In 1852, 167 reported a combined capital of $241,000 and sales of $1,696,000.

The next year internal difficulties arose to plague the movement. The stores did much of their buying through the central purchasing agency in Boston, of which John Kaulback was manager. The agency was controlled by a "Board of Trade" on which the local Unions were represented. Certain groups were dissatisfied with Kaulback and persuaded the board of trade to discharge him. His friends resented this. They withdrew from the New England Protective Union and organized a rival organization called the American Protective Union.

The new organization soon outgrew its parent. Four years after the split it boasted 327 local societies whose total investment of $290,000 supported an annual trade of $2,000,000. The 327 stores were scattered in some ten different states.

The New England Union had 63 active stores whose total capital and sales were about half those of its rival.

1857 was high tide for the movement. In thirteen years over 700 local stores had been set up. Many failed, but most of them were able to liquidate in an orderly manner with their affairs in reasonable condition. Some 400 were carrying on what seemed a successful program of merchandising.

1858 brought its conclusive evidence of decline. A few months of uncertain prices upset the calculations of managers and directors, discouraged the faint-hearted, and led directly to many liquidations. Competing business had learned to adjust its prices to Protective Union levels. This wiped out most of the apparent advantages to the consumers and caused many to lose interest. Finally the shadows of a great war diverted the attention of men and women from their bread and butter problems. Unit at a time, the movement waned.

When the war was over, a few stores remained in existence. By 1890 only three were left: one at Natick, one at Worcester, in Massachusetts, and one at Salmon Falls, New Hampshire.

America's first great consumers' co-operative effort failed. It was inevitably so. The Protective Union had no precedents to guide it. Its leaders made a stab in the dark. The story of the Rochdale Pioneers was an untold tale. The saving device of

avoiding price wars by charging market prices and paying refunds to the consumers was then an obscure English invention.

The Protective Unions were quite like the Union Shops promoted by Dr. King. They operated much like them and failed through similar mistakes. They did survive longer and grew larger. America did better with her first attempt at establishing consumer-owned stores than did England. Unfortunately, such cannot be said for later efforts.

The first Rochdale co-operative established on American soil was located at Lawrence, Massachusetts. It began operations in 1863 on a capital of $1,400. It flourished for a few years, but eventually died.

The second extensive wave of consumers' co-operative activity came after the war. It was a child of the inevitable post-war depression. When the tragic conflict between the North and South was over it left the economics of the nation out of joint. The vanquished territory had been ravished. The northern states had an overexpanded industry geared to the destructive needs of Mars.

When the soldiers were mustered out of the armies they went home to a northern labor market, already glutted, or to a devastated and impoverished southern agriculture. In an effort to start life anew many of them set their faces westward to take homesteads on the virgin acres of Iowa, Minnesota, the

Dakotas, Kansas, Nebraska, and Oklahoma. They were joined in this move by unemployed industrial workers and by a wave of immigrants who swept into the United States as soon as the war was over.

Rich land fertilized by human toil yielded bumper crops. The agricultural production of the nation swept to a new high and the prices of farm products hit a toboggan. Those who had worked hard to give the world more food were rewarded for their effort with privation and in many cases loss of their land. Many a homesteader had borrowed at high rates of interest to get his stake in the world only to find himself closed out when the land became his, because he could not pay his debts. The sheriffs' hammers beat a tattoo up and down the American frontier.

Hardship fell not on the pioneers alone. The farmers of New England and the other eastern states found it hard to compete with the more fertile and productive western lands. They shared in the general agricultural depression.

Against these hardships the farmers rebelled. They resented the fact that often the railroads got more for hauling produce to market than the producer received for all his work. They claimed it was unjust to have to pay debts incurred when wheat sold for more than a dollar a bushel with grain worth half its former price. They felt it was unfair for manufacturers to keep up their prices amid the general suffering.

So when Oliver Hudson Kelley, founder of the great agricultural fraternity, "The Patrons of Husbandry" or Grange, went out to organize the farmers of America he found them ready and waiting. The Granger movement became prairie fire.

This secret order was the direct result of Kelley's concern over the post-war conditions among farmers. Shortly after the war he had been sent out by the national government to study conditions. He found them so disheartening that he resolved to set up an organization to give farmers a greater sense of the dignity of their profession and to make them more skillful as tillers of the soil.

The first local or "subordinate" Grange was established in 1868 at Fredonia, New York. Others followed in Minnesota, Wisconsin, Ohio, Indiana, Illinois, Iowa, Kansas. During the early seventies Granges were chartered by the hundreds. By January 1, 1875, the United States had over 21,000 of them acting as rally centers for embittered and embattled farmers.

In 1869 the Minnesota State Grange took action to establish a state exchange to assist subordinates in the buying and selling of goods. News of this step spread rapidly. Soon the Grangers' resentment against their treatment in the market place expressed itself in programs of co-operative buying and selling. The selling program never advanced very far but it wasn't long until co-operative purchasing was a part of the activities of nearly every local group.

There was no uniformity to their plan of operations. Some established stores financed through the sale of shares to members, a great many more appointed local purchasing agents who pooled orders for supplies, bought them at wholesale, and passed them on to the consumers at a small margin of profit. In a few cases, particularly in Illinois, the Grange at first stayed out of the commodity business and encouraged its membership to join with other groups in the establishment of stores to serve all the rural population.

The business program aroused great enthusiasm. The farmers believed that it was to be salvation in the midst of their pressing difficulties. The interest is reflected in the cold figures of Grange business records. Iowa led the field with a volume of $5,000,000 in 1873; Indiana did a wholesale business alone which exceeded $300,000 in 1875; the Ohio State Grange purchased over $100,000 worth of groceries from one wholesale house in 1878; the Maryland warehouse handled goods whose value totaled $358,000 in 1877. Just one of the joint ventures in Illinois did a $100,000 business in 1873. This was the largest in the state but several others were in existence during the first half of the seventies.

After an almost phenomenal initial success with its business program the Grange began to have a sharp decline in membership. The root cause was weaknesses in the commercial activities. The National Grange gave no guidance to the farmers' desire to co-operate until 1875. Each local and state organization did about what was right in its own eyes. What seemed right was usually wrong. This was particularly true with the price policy. The whole initial emphasis was on saving money. It was a natural emphasis for a people in serious plight financially but it was a fatal one.

Where stores were established it got them involved in price wars which they could ill afford. Where the business agent system was maintained prices were often put so low that they did not cover the actual cost of doing business. This resulted in false conceptions of value which sometimes had weird effects. In 1878 the Ohio business agent complained because local Granges objected to a one and one-half per cent commission necessary to make the wholesale program break even.

The results of these policies began to make themselves felt in 1874. The first state to feel them was Iowa. Her state Grange launched a farm machinery factory which promptly went into bankruptcy. This brought on the virtual collapse of the Granger movement in the state. Other states followed in short order.

The peak of membership was January 1875. At that time there were over 21,000 local bodies of the order. A year and one-half later the number had shrunk to a bare 15,000.

Much of this decline might have been avoided had the National Grange concerned itself with the commercial program earlier. But it was not until 1875 that a sound plan of co-operation was brought forward. During the year previous the national officials had made contact with the English co-operators, mastered the Rochdale plan, and come to believe in it implicitly. The 1875 national convention of the order endorsed it. Following this action pamphlets were printed and distributed asking local Granges to adopt the English practices. Every effort was made to reorganize the consumers' co-operative program on a sound basis.

In 1876 the national body went even further. It approved a plan for covering this country with Grange-sponsored Rochdale co-operative societies, the establishment of a national wholesale to supply them with goods, and the creation of an Anglo-American co-operative exchange to serve both the English Co-operative Wholesale Society and the proposed Grange wholesale.

Thus for the first time in American history a comprehensive program for establishing the consumers' co-operative movement was approved by a great farmers' organization. But the plan never

got past the blueprint stage. The rapid decline in membership of the order during the remainder of the decade rendered it impotent. Nothing the National officials could do arrested the decline. The Grange and co-operation had become almost synonymous in the thinking of many farmers. When the initial co-operative efforts failed they usually had no inclination to try again on a basis imported from another country.

However, in the areas into which the Grange had been slow to expand during the first half of the decade a goodly number of stores were established on the proven plan. This was particularly true in parts of the South and in New England. Mention has already been made of the Maryland state exchange. It was supported by Rochdale stores and operated successfully for a number of years. In 1878 the Texas Co-operative Association was established with a capital of $250. In ten years its capital exceeded $50,000. Its annual volume of business exceeded one-half million. It served as wholesale for a number of local societies. There were 92 of these in 1882 and 150 in 1887.

Around 1880 the Grange established stores in Maine, New Hampshire, Massachusetts, Connecticut, New York, Pennsylvania, and Delaware. Most of these survived for a full decade. One remains today. It is located at Jay, Maine, and has several hundred members.

Kansas was involved in the great decline of 1876 but the co-operative program was rebuilt to some extent thereafter. A Rochdale store was set up in Johnson county in that year. It grew until its volume was a third of a million dollars per annum. Its success led to the establishment of between thirty and forty other stores in the state. They survived until the closing years of the century.

But eventually most of the later Grange co-operatives of the nineteenth century failed. The American farmer was not yet ready for co-operation.

The farmer was not unique in that respect. People in other occupations had just as little inclination for group business activity. The history of two other waves of co-operative interest bears its convincing testimony to that fact.

Shortly after the Granger movement got under way a second secret order of significance to the social historian appeared on the scene: the Sovereigns of Industry. William H. Earle of Worcester, Massachusetts, was its founder.

He was a schoolmate of Dudley W. Adams who became Master of the National Grange in 1873. Adams asked him to become state organizer of Massachusetts, but he refused because of a stubborn conviction that an organization made up of farmers alone could not solve the ills of human society.

Earle was acutely conscious of the common needs of the human race whether farmers, professional

workers, or industrial laborers. He believed in the Grange type of organization but wanted an order open to men of all classes. This led to the founding of the Sovereigns of Industry in 1874.

In its preamble were these words: "It will present organized resistance to the monopolies and other evils of the existing industrial and commercial system. It will try to establish a better system of economical exchanges, and to promote, on the basis of equity and liberty, mutual fellowship and co-operative action among the producers and consumers of wealth throughout the earth."

Stripped of its high sounding phrases the program was to establish consumers' co-operative societies. The first store was opened by the order at Springfield, Massachusetts, in 1874. By 1877 ninety-four "councils"—as the local organizations were called—reported a total business volume of $1,089,372 with net earnings of $152,000. Stores were located as far west as Akron, Ohio.

The Springfield store was the only one which did not operate on the Rochdale basis. It got started on the familiar price cutting program but abandoned it in 1877. The officers of the National Council constantly emphasized the importance of following the methods so successfully used by the English co-operators. The organizational pamphlet gave specific and unmistakable instruction at this point.

But nevertheless the stores failed. The order itself had ceased to exist by 1880.

A fourth attempt at consumers' co-operation was made during the nineteenth century by America's first Industrial Union: the Noble Order of the Knights of Labor—the nation's first CIO. For a decade the history of organized labor was the history of this secret society. It was the first national American union not organized on a craft basis. Carpenters, bricklayers, telegraph operators, packing-house workers, miners were alike welcome in its "Assemblies." This lusty organization grew to power in the days when the Morgans, Rockefellers, McCormicks, and Vanderbilts were laying the foundations of their great empires of finance and industry. It was wrecked on *steel*.

The order was founded by Uriah Smith Stevens, a tailor by trade who was educated for the ministry and who was for a time a school teacher. He was a disciple of the Christian Socialists of England and wrote into the ritual of the Knights his devotion to producers' and consumers' co-operation. In the beginning these things received great emphasis but eventually the rank and file became much more interested in ordinary collective bargaining with better wages and shorter hours as the goal and the strike and the boycott as weapons.

These more violent tactics got results for a time. So powerful did the organization become that even

Jay Gould recognized it as the bargaining agency for railroad men rather than risk a general strike on his roads. That was in 1885. One year later the order stood at the zenith of its power with over 700,000 members.

Decline came when an alienated public opinion turned against it, and supported the steel barons in their stern resolve to preserve the open-shop principle. The public changed its sympathies when local assemblies lost their sense of responsibility and wildcat striking seemed to threaten the orderliness of industrial processes. The 700,000 members of 1886 had shrunk to a mere 100,000 by 1890.

But while they majored in strikes the Knights of Labor minored in co-operatives. They started at least 185 producers' co-operatives, in which men banded themselves together as craftsmen to make and market together the things their hands created. Many of the Assemblies operated stores. It was not at all unusual to find two-story labor halls in which the first floor was occupied by a co-operative store while the second provided a meeting place for the union.

These stores were always strictly Knights of Labor projects. They gave special discounts to members of the order. The profits were used to swell strike war-chests or help with the extensive mutual aid program of the organization. When the order declined the stores languished. They left little behind them—not even records to be investigated by co-operative historians interested in post-mortems.

Besides the four movements described in this chapter there were a host of minor efforts to make the consumers' co-operative principle work. American labor leaders were constantly in touch with the doings of their English brethren. They preached the importance of consumer action. There were the ever present group of idealists who accepted co-operation as a superior pattern of business to competitive capitalism. They advocated the movement with both vigor and enthusiasm. Many co-operatives were started in various sections of the country during the century but they were all hothouse plants. They would flourish in the heat of first enthusiasm but showed little ability to survive in the hurly-burly economics of a pioneering country.

Americans were too busy conquering a continent to worry much about their problems as consumers.

CHAPTER VIII

Via Finland and Bohemia

WITH THE COMING of the present century new streams of population came flowing into the great Melting Pot. Bohemians and Finns began to leave their native land for America. By 1910 a goodly number of both peoples were here. Two new tongues were added to the babble of voices; more important, a new stream of influence flowed into the torrent of American economic life. These two peoples were co-operators. They brought the knowledge of Rochdale practice with them. Where they settled, store societies came into being, struggled for a few years, and then leaped forward to real success. The Finns settled in Massachusetts, Minnesota, Wisconsin, northern Michigan, Illinois, and New Jersey; the Bohemians in Ohio and Illinois.

The oldest and strongest of the Bohemian societies is at Dillonvale, in the heart of southeastern Ohio's coal region. It started in 1908 in a little two-by-four building built by the members' own hands. In 1909 its total business was $12,572.53. The first patronage refund was paid in 1911. It was $279.95. Since then there has been steady growth. Today the only brick business block in Dillonvale is the property of this old society which calls itself the New Co-operative Company. It dominates the trade of the community.

Branch stores are located in a number of surrounding towns and mining camps. Wherever they are found they give the toiling miners excellent food at reasonable prices and freedom from the tyranny of the company store. In 1933 a quarter century of successful business operation was celebrated. The volume then was more than a quarter million per year. In 1937 total sales were $753,870.18.

The New Co-operative Company is more than a business enterprise. It is a great experiment, demonstrating what people can do for themselves in the midst of adverse economic conditions. It has been a bulwark of defense for the miners in their struggles against the coal companies. It has enriched cultural life. Its musical organizations offer real opportunities for artistic self-expression. Its club rooms are the heart of community social life. Membership is now made up of many nationalities. It serves not only the miners but also the farmers of the surrounding countryside.

One of the strongest of the societies of Finnish origin is the Co-operative Trading Company of Waukegan, Illinois. It began in 1910. The initial cause was an increase in the price of milk. Milk dealers had decided to charge eight instead of six cents per quart for milk. Protests were in vain.

Finally an incensed group of Finnish housewives decided to route their resentment into constructive channels. They formed a buying club and started purchasing milk direct from a farmer. They sold milk for six cents a quart and still made a small margin of profit.

This activity on the part of the women stimulated the interest of the men. They decided to set up a co-operative. On May 5, 1911, sixty-two persons of Swedish and Finnish extraction incorporated the Co-operative Dairy. A capital of $630 was subscribed. The equipment of a private dealer was purchased for $500. The consumers started the processing of milk for themselves.

The first year's sales were $6,810, on which there was a net loss of $74. This small loss was redeemed the next year. Membership had grown to 101; capital to $1,008; sales had doubled. There followed three very successful years, but in 1918 the bookkeeper was forced to use red ink again—to record a loss of $22.56 on a business volume of $37,110. The next year the volume jumped to over $100,000 but the loss was $5,658. The directors burned midnight oil working out plans for reorganization. In 1920 things were on an even keel again. A volume of $183,078 resulted in an earning of $8,243. Since that time the bookkeeper has been able to leave the cork in the red ink bottle. In 1935 the business volume was $631,408, the share capital totaled

$72,140, the membership was 2,062, the net earnings were $19,345.28. In 1937 annual sales were more than $800,000.

Not only is this organization operating a successful dairy, it maintains a bakery and operates six grocery stores and meat markets. In 1936 it built a beautiful filling station on a prominent corner of the city and launched into the distribution of petroleum products.

This business has been built up in the face of the bitterest kind of competition. Waukegan is full of chain stores which have crowded the independent dealers to the wall. But the co-operative has thrived in the face of the competition. It is the one hope for maintaining local ownership of the food distributing business.

Stores of Finnish origin are the thickest in Minnesota, Wisconsin, and northern Michigan. Here these hardy people settled in greatest numbers. In the heart of their communities they planted co-operatives. One of the oldest of these was organized in 1908 at Nashwauk, Minnesota. It was called the Elanto Company—an American echo of the then three-year-old Elanto society of Helsingfors.

Severe struggles marked the early years of most of the organizations in this territory but a people schooled to hardships in their fatherland were not daunted by them in their adopted country. In July 1917 representatives from 19 struggling stores came together at Superior, Wisconsin, to discuss their mutual woes. One of the very real difficulties was securing goods. Private wholesales discriminated against the co-operators. The only answer seemed to be a co-operative wholesale.

In order to get the venture under way a collection was taken which totaled $15.50. It wasn't much but it was enough to make a beginning. With few physical assets save a desk and a rebuilt typewriter the Central Co-operative Wholesale began business operations on September 1.

When the books were audited, at the end of that year, sales totaled $25,573. There were 15 member societies. The total share capital was $580. Net earnings were $268.06—all of which was added to the capital of the business. In 1920 member societies had grown to 44, and 58 others were doing some business with the wholesale. That year its volume was $409,590; the net worth had grown to $21,911. Ten years later it was serving 137 societies. In 1937 its business volume was $3,356,550.

While the Finnish and Bohemian immigrants were forging out America's first significant consumers' co-operative successes native Americans were making history of another sort. The first two decades of the twentieth century continued the dismal records of failure which characterized the nineteenth.

Americans have refused to believe that co-operation would not work here. They have tried it again and again. At no time was their persistence more evident than from 1900 to 1920. As will be shown later, farmers launched ambitious co-operative programs during these years. Other occupational groups were not far behind.

California was one of the places where a large body of consumers went into business for themselves. Illinois was another.

A co-operative wholesale called the Rochdale Wholesale Society was started in 1900 in San Francisco. It was set up by leaders of a number of local societies which had established stores during the five years previous. The Rochdale Society was created to provide co-operatives with a source of supply for goods and to carry on educational work in the state. It gave constant encouragement to community groups wanting to start stores. By 1905 there were 51 local societies owning shares of stock in the wholesale. These had an average membership of 100 families. They did a combined business of about $4,000,000 per year. In addition the state had 17 consumers' co-operatives not a part of the Rochdale federation. 1906 was a year of expansion. Over 30 new societies were organized in the state. But most of these were of the hot-house variety and the severe economic depression of 1907 wiped out many of them. By 1910 over half the "Rochdale" stores had failed. Ten more went under during 1910.

In order to save the situation a complete reorganization was attempted. A state-wide society called the Pacific Co-operative League was formed. Local organizations were absorbed in it. Stores were taken over and operated as branches of the central body which gave them some local self-government but maintained a fairly rigid supervision. The League insisted on conservative business practices and proper bookkeeping methods. It set up an auditing service, maintained a legal department to help its local affiliates, and carried on an extensive educational and organizational program.

This move injected new life into the California development. By 1921 the League was operating 47 stores in California, Nevada, New Mexico, and Arizona. Its membership exceeded 15,000 and its annual sales were better than $4,000,000. But in the very year of its greatest financial success it ceased to be *co-operative*.

The maintenance of democratic control is always a problem when a co-operative attempts to serve too wide a territory. The Pacific League was operating in four states. The membership simply could not get together to elect directors and officials. So in 1921 the insiders took the the program over. The democratic principle was abolished: 51 per cent of the voting stock was given to three trustees.

There was an immediate and wholly justified reaction from the customers. The League was forced into receivership in 1922. By 1925 California had but 12 stores. Within 9 years as many of these had failed. Finally just three remained to join the procession of post-depression co-operatives.

Illinois wrote a tale not unlike that of California. In the closing years of the nineteenth century a citizen of St. Louis, N. O. Nelson by name, became very much interested in co-operatives. He was intimate with the Christian Socialists of England and was the one American to attend the first meeting of the International Co-operative Alliance. His contacts with the devoted but mistaken leaders of the English Co-operative Union led him to think in terms of *profit-sharing*. He came home and put his ideas into effect in the factory which he owned at Edwardsville, Illinois. He encouraged his employees to organize a consumers' society. This was the LeClaire Co-operative Society of Edwardsville which closed twenty-five years of history by failing in 1925. In 1902 he attempted to rally the scattered societies of the United States into a national federation but without success.

In the meantime the city of Chicago was the birthplace of a peculiar co-operative development. It was not exactly a consumers' organization, for the majority of its stockholders were private merchants. It was called the "Co-operative Merchants Company." 1900 was the date of its organization. Shares were sold for $10 each in blocks of 20. Over 400 stores purchased the minimum holding required. Most of them were privately owned but there was a sprinkling of co-operatives among them. Evidently not all the American merchant class were afraid of the consumer-owned store. The company promised 8 per cent interest on capital. Earnings in excess of this were to be divided among the patrons in proportion to purchases.

Shortly afterward the leaders of the Co-operative Merchants Company started the Right Relationship League for the purpose of encouraging co-operative stores. Organizers were sent out to foster interest in them. They went into a community which promised support, sold shares at $100 each, promising 8 per cent interest. The money was used to buy the store of some friendly local merchant who became the manager of the new consumer-owned enterprise. The stores were expected to use the Merchants Co-operative as a source of supply.

In 1904 the League called a national co-operative congress in St. Louis. Enthusiastic individuals proposed a national co-operative league which would establish standardized Rochdale stores all over the United States. This grandiose proposal exhausted itself in oratory. In 1908 the Right Relationship League decided that Illinois was unappreciative of its efforts and moved to Minneapolis.

While these ambitious schemes were going forward a few stores grew out of the grass roots of human need. The first was the Lombard Society

Store established by Italian miners of Herrin in 1901. Thrifty Scotch followed suit at Glen Carbon in 1904. By the close of 1905 there were ten societies in the state: at Herrin, Glen Carbon, Bloomington, Edwardsville, Champaign, Chicago, Marion, Pana, Sesser, and Waukegan. The largest was the McLean County Co-operative of Bloomington.

By this time the Illinois Miners' Union had become well established among the coal men of the state. Its leadership was enthusiastically committed to the idea that securing higher wages and shorter hours alone offered no solution to the workers' problems. They believed that consumer action was also necessary and were unceasing in urging the miners to establish co-operative stores. John H. Walker, president of the Illinois Federation of Labor, and Duncan McDonald, secretary of the United Mine Workers, were both ardent co-operators.

By 1915 the total number of stores in the state had grown to 32. By 1916 the time seemed ripe for the establishment of some sort of federation. Representatives from 21 societies met at Staunton and organized the Central States Co-operative Association. The need for a wholesale was discussed but shelved in favor of carrying on a temporary joint-buying program.

This expedient worked very well until 1918 when it was replaced by the Central States Wholesale

Society with headquarters at East St. Louis. It was created to serve some 50 societies located in various parts of the state but concentrated in the southern coal belt. Sales for the first month were more than $5,000; for the second more than $10,000. This organization might have grown slowly into importance and usefulness—as did the Central Wholesale of Superior—had not some of the leaders of the state decided to improve on Rochdale methods. They designed what was called the American Rochdale plan. It was quite American.

The American Rochdale plan was expected to put co-operation over in a big way. Instead of waiting for the stirring of the grass roots to result in the establishment of local societies, a plan for establishing co-operative chain-stores was launched. Funds for the venture came from the treasury of the Miners' Union. The Wholesale was made the daddy of an illegitimate brood of 70 stores which were not locally owned but which were the property of the central organization. By 1922 the Miners' Union had poured over $400,000 into this effort.

With academic and typically American enthusiasm a professor of the University of Illinois wrote to the sponsors of this idea: "I believe you have started something that is going to be one of the biggest things on the continent." The manager of the enterprise waxed eloquent in 1920: "Before the year is out we will have stores in every labor center in

Illinois. . . . I believe that the American Rochdale Plan will be running in every town in the United States before five years." The professor was right—it turned out to be one of the biggest co-operative *failures* on the continent.

The chain-store idea was not the only feature of the plan. Another American improvement was the abandonment of the current market-price policy and repayment of overcharges in the form of a patron's dividend. The stores cut prices from the start in order "to let the customer carry home his dividend with his groceries." By 1922 the whole bubble had burst. Losses wiped out virtually the entire capital investment.

Efforts at rebuilding on the plodding technique of the Pioneers were in vain. The collapse carried down not only the wholesale and its branches but many of the stores which had started on the proven basis. Only a handful of societies survived.

At about the time all this was happening in Illinois, the miners of western Pennsylvania began setting up stores. Around 1918 a federation called the Tri-State Co-operative Society was formed at Pittsburgh. It operated for a time simply as a wholesale and educational organization. Then it became afflicted with the chain-store idea. By 1919 it had 23 branch stores in operation.

Around Seattle a movement got under way in 1918. It grew like wildfire for a time. In 1918 there was a wholesale operating in St. Paul with the name "The Co-operative Wholesale of America." It had about 75 affiliated stores in Minnesota and the Dakotas. This same year witnessed an effort to create a national wholesale to serve all of America through the operation of branches in various regions. The entire co-operative movement of the nation—excepting the Finlanders and Bohemians—seemed afflicted with megalomania. Everybody wanted to do something big.

This all-American wholesale was incorporated in 1919 as the National Co-operative Association. Its capitalization was put at $1,000,000. The plan called for the taking over of five wholesales located in various parts of the country. The details were never worked out but branches were set up in Seattle, Hoboken, and Chicago. The chain-store idea was tried at all three places. By 1921 the whole venture had become a bad memory. Its collapse left its residue of co-operative wreckage to be buried along with the efforts of the nineteenth century.

In the meantime one venture in co-operative federation had been started which was destined to continue. That was the formation of a national educational union whose purpose was not to operate business, but to give guidance to old and new societies —to spread the knowledge of co-operation among the American people.

On March 18, 1916, a small group of enthusiastic

co-operators met at 384 Washington Avenue, Brooklyn, and approved a constitution for the Co-operative League of the U. S. A. The first executive secretary was Scott H. Perky who served it on a full time basis without compensation. The first president was Dr. James Peter Warbasse, an eminent surgeon who was vitally interested in the ills of human society as well as the ills of the human body. The first offices were located at 70 Fifth Avenue, New York City. Dr. Warbasse has continued president through the years. The offices have since been moved to 167 West 12th St.

Immediately after it was organized the League began the publication of literature. It took over an all but extinct monthly magazine called *The Co-operative Consumer* and made it the official organ. In the first year four pamphlets were produced: "The Co-operative League—Its Aims and Principles," "Consumers' Co-operation, the Mass Movement," "Constitution of the Co-operative League," and "Consumers' Co-operation during the War." A survey of the existing societies was begun. In 1918 a study of failures was published as a guide away from difficulties. In 1917 a technical advisory board was created. This was followed by a speakers' bureau and a news bureau. This same year the American Federation of Labor became interested in co-operatives and spent considerable sums of money promoting the movement among labor groups.

In 1918 there appeared a book *Co-operation—the Hope of the Consumer* by Emerson P. Harris. It was one of the first American publications on the subject. It was followed in 1919 by Albert Sonnichsen's monumental volume *Consumers' Co-operation*.

The League called the first national congress of co-operators at Springfield, Illinois. It met in September 1918. About three hundred people were present. This first congress was characterized by optimism and enthusiasm—in fact a little too much of both, for out of this gathering came the resolve to form the National Co-operative Association. In the beginning some encouragement was given to this venture. It was a mistake which League officials soon had occasion to regret. The second national congress, held in Cincinnati in 1920, was characterized by controversy over the affairs of this still-born wholesale. Naturally its failure and that of the Central States Wholesale were severe blows to American co-operation.

But the League went ahead undaunted, resolved to profit by the mistakes of those whose mania for bigness led them into disastrous over-expansion.

In 1921 affiliation with the International Co-operative Alliance was effected. Thus the American movement became a part of the world co-operative fellowship. Dr. and Mrs. Warbasse were sent as delegates to the International congress held that year at Basle, Switzerland. The third congress was held in Chicago in 1922; the fourth in New York in 1924. By that time there were 333 societies affiliated with it. Their total membership was about fifty thousand and their volume of business nearly $15,000,000. The fiascoes of the early twenties were forgotten and the outlook for a steady and healthy progress seemed good.

However, the next five years were anything but encouraging. By 1926 the number of affiliated societies had decreased. Urban America was sick with a feverish prosperity. The New Era, publicized by Coolidge and Hoover, was getting into full swing. Credit was free and easy, stockmarket gambling had become a national pastime, installment buying had become the great American habit. America was getting rich by going into debt. Interest in the plodding methods of co-operation hit a slump. By 1928 the number of societies in the League had dropped to 138. They did, however, represent an aggregate membership of 77,843.

Three regional federations had come into being to supplement the work of the national League. The oldest of these was the Northern States Co-operative League with headquarters at Minneapolis. It had been organized in 1922. The Finnish societies formed the backbone of its membership. The territory of this organization was North and South Dakota, Wisconsin, Minnesota, and upper Michigan.

In 1930 it could report 31 affiliated societies. The Eastern States League came in 1924. In 1930 it had 24 affiliated societies which included the Eastern Co-operative Wholesale, organized by ten local groups in 1929. The Central States Co-operative League with headquarters at Bloomington, Illinois, came into being in 1926. It reported thirteen member societies in 1930. Its territory was Ohio, Indiana, lower Michigan, and Illinois. (The offices of the Central States League are now at Chicago. A wholesale was set up in connection with it in 1936.)

The foreign-language societies formed the backbone of both the national and regional leagues. The Finnish societies had been making a steady growth but in 1930 political difficulties had come to a head in many of them. The Communists had tried to get control. That issue had to be faced at the congress held at Superior in that year. It was settled by an emphatic declaration of political neutrality. A few societies under Communist domination noisily pulled out.

Surveyed from the vantage point of 1929 and from the records of the League the co-operative picture was pretty dismal. The facts seemed to say that America was not the soil in which co-operative effort could thrive. Eighty-five years of failure lay in the background. The earlier failures could be rightly attributed to ignorance of efficient techniques. The pre-Civil War co-operators knew nothing of the Rochdale story. The Protective Union movement, like the Union Shop movement of England, was a stab in the dark. It lived longer and grew larger than the corresponding English development but eventually went the same route. The Grangers didn't discover Rochdale practices until it was too late to save their business organizations.

Those who were back of the American Rochdale plan and the National Co-operative Association knew the story of the English development but they could not resist the temptation to try something different. Back of their behavior was something of the anti-foreign complex of the American who refuses to believe he can learn anything from the old world, and insists that there is nothing from other lands that cannot be bettered by something typically American.

The efforts at chain-store co-operation were typically American. It was designed to do things quickly and in large proportions. America has been a land of quick growth. Small towns have grown into cities in just a few years. Little businesses have become industrial giants in the lifetime of one man. The nation itself had expanded from thirteen seaboard colonies to a world power in a century and a half. Perhaps it was too much to expect that American co-operators would not be affected by what they observed all about them in private business.

But even this love of speed and great size does

not account for all failures. It cannot explain the decline of societies from 1920 to 1929. It does not tell why the Rochdale societies which survived the Grange collapse never grew to great importance. Co-operatives languished here fundamentally because Americans had other ways of solving their economic difficulties. There was no deep-rooted need for co-operatives.

Vast and unexploited natural resources were constantly inviting daring men to exploit them. Land was easily available. The farmer who lost one farm could homestead and get another. When New England soil fertility was exhausted the western plains became dotted with New England families. There was no reason to stay at home and solve problems by hard and painstaking labor. It was easier to run away from poverty. Free land offered quick results. If a job was lost, usually another was easily found. If a temporary depression came, a spectacular boom followed—likewise temporary, but it made it easy to forget. An expanding industrialism was labor-hungry. The millions from Europe poured in because manpower was needed. This was an expanding nation whose conquest of a continent kept most hands busy at fairly good wages.

It was easy to climb in America. The boy born in a cabin could become the president of the United States. The boy born poor could become rich. That fact kept all the poor working in the hope that they might achieve affluence. The majority were doomed to defeat in the struggle for wealth but that fact did nothing to lessen the competition for individual achievement. It merely sharpened men's resolves to outdo others.

These are the things which have kept America from being a nation of co-operators. This has been a frontier country. Her history has been a story of great conquest. The frontiers are now at an end. The westward movement of people has been stopped by the Pacific Ocean. Homesteads have all been taken. Free lands are no more.

CHAPTER IX

The Farmer Takes a Hand

UNTIL THE LATE depression wrought its devastating work on the essential individualism of the American city dweller, consumers' co-operation could not get under way in our industrial communities. It has made headway among the American rural people. Their depression started with the close of the World War. Its bitter lessons were being learned before the events following 1929 disturbed the social and economic life of the nation. The farmers—often regarded as incapable of co-operative action—have taken the lead in giving to the United States her largest and most successful consumer organizations. Nearly all of them are children of the present century and most of them were born during the last two decades.

Some have been sponsored by the three large farmers' membership organizations—Grange, Farmers Union, and Farm Bureau. Some have grown up independently, out of the felt need for lower prices and better quality consumer goods. Others arrived as marketing organizations, came to see that it is not enough to get the farmer more for what he sells. The solution of his problem demands the protection of his interest as a consumer as well.

Of the membership organizations, the Grange is the oldest. During the seventies and the eighties it tried to teach the farmers of America to buy and sell together. But that lesson came too early. The close of the frontier had not yet prepared the social soil for the planting of the co-operative idea. When conditions were favorable, this agricultural fraternity began where it left off in the eighties with a new program of co-operative purchasing. This was particularly true in the far northwest. Previous to 1920 the Washington State Grange launched a program of establishing what were called "Grange Warehouse Associations." When the United States Bureau of Labor Statistics surveyed the consumers' co-operative picture in the United States in 1920 it found 51 such organizations in the state. In 1918 the Grange Co-operative Wholesale was established at Seattle. The program has since grown to substantial size. Today there are 73 local co-operatives identified with it. In 1936 the wholesale volume was $1,800,000. In 1937 it was 30 per cent greater. Farm supplies, petroleum products, and groceries are handled.

In other states the Grange carries on some commercial activities but not through local co-operatives. Business agents, local and state, sell commodities to members. In some areas co-operation is encouraged as a general practice. Members are left free to unite with their neighbors in whatever type of project it seems best to support.

The Farmers Union was born in 1902 at Point, Texas. Probably the oldest consumers' co-operative started by this group, and still in operation, is the Rogers Mill County Co-operative Association of Oklahoma. It was formed in 1905. Its membership today is 250; its capital and surplus $73,000.

However, in its first years, the Farmers Co-operative and Educational Union did not establish many such organizations. It did what the early Granges had done: appointed purchasing agents in its locals through whom its members could pool their orders. In time the ineffectiveness of this method became apparent. By 1919 Rochdale principles received the official endorsement of the National Union. An ambitious and far-reaching program of setting up stores was launched. By 1920 nearly 600 had been established in 19 different states. Nebraska topped the list with 204; Kansas followed with 177; Kentucky was a poor third with 18.

Kansas and Nebraska both established state buying organizations in 1914. In the beginning the Nebraska Farmers Union Exchange was not a co-operative. It was like the early Grange business agencies—a department of the membership organization through which Farmers Union locals could route their purchases. In 1916 this setup was abandoned. The Nebraska Farmers Union State Exchange was incorporated as a state-wide co-operative in which any Farmers Union member in the territory could hold shares. Nearly 7,000 people subscribed a total of $719,000 capital to get it under way. This super co-operative was to be a wholesale for locals and a mail-order house for individuals. In 1919 the chain-store idea was tried. Branch stores were set up in sections where adequate local financing was forthcoming. If the farmers of a community wanted a store they had to subscribe to enough capital in the State Exchange to pay for it. Management was not under local control, however. This setup was just getting nicely started when the depression of 1920 began.

During 1919 an overeager management had purchased large stocks of goods at high prices. These had to be sold at a loss or not sold at all. For four straight years money was lost. By 1923 one-half the capital of the organization had been wiped out. These losses were written off in 1925 by halving the value of the shares.

The disasters which hit the state exchange likewise affected local organization. By 1925 only 104 out of the 204 stores, in existence in 1920, remained in operation. But that year was a turning point. Farmers Union members resolved to rebuild. Since that time there has been steady progress. Today 260 Farmers Union stores use the Exchange as a wholesale. Fifteen of these are managed by it—survivors of the chain-store set-up. The rest are locally owned and controlled. The assets have been rebuilt to $750,000. In 1935 its sales totaled $2,604,532.10. The merchandise handled included groceries, fruits, vegetables, work clothing, shoes, school supplies, farm machinery, hardware, fencing, twine, seeds, paints, oils, greases, gasoline, kerosene, and fertilizer.

Kansas went in for long names and called its Farmers Union wholesale "the Jobbing Association of the Kansas Branch of the National Farmers Educational and Co-operative Union." Much printer's ink has been saved by shortening the name to "Farmers Union Jobbing Association." The original capital was $20,000.

Co-operation flourished in Kansas for a time. 1920 was a high point. Then followed half a decade of disaster. Nearly half the local stores failed. Serious losses were incurred by the wholesale. Signs of new vitality began to show themselves in 1927. Since then nearly 400 stores have been established. The annual volume of the Jobbing Association is now well past the million dollar mark.

Oklahoma boasts some 100 Farmers Union Co-ops. Most of these are cotton-ginning associations which do a supply business on the side. In 1936 the receipts from ginning operations totaled more than $1,000,000; sales of farm supplies were about 25 per cent less. Nine co-operative oil associations, distributing petroleum products, were in existence at that time and the number has since increased. She is not an outstanding state from the standpoint of the number and size of the co-operatives within her borders, but she is unique in having the nation's first co-operative hospital. This institution located at Elk City is providing its member families with a complete health service for $25 per year plus certain nominal additional charges for surgery, special nursing, obstetrics, and other unusual things. The doctors and other staff members are on salary. To become a member of the hospital association a family must invest $50 in shares which is used for buildings and equipment. The medical association of the state hasn't been too friendly toward the idea of having those who use the services own the hospital but in spite of opposition from this source the organization flourishes.

The largest Farmers Union co-operative wholesale is the baby of the lot, founded in 1927 at St. Paul, Minnesota. It serves 240 local associations, 94 of which are in North Dakota, 68 in Montana, 36 in Wisconsin, and 34 in Minnesota. In 1937 the volume was more than $4,500,000.

This whole development was built on ruins. The Farmers Union was very active in the Old Northwest previous to 1916. It had established some co-operatives. They all failed when A. C. Townley appeared on the scene and organized the Non-Partisan League. He persuaded the farmers that all their difficulties could be solved by militant political action. When the League was able to gain control of both the Democrat and Republican political machinery in North Dakota, co-operatives died from neglect. The Farmers Union was forgotten in the excitement. When, after about seven years of victory and final defeat, the Non-Partisan League passed out of existence, farm leaders painfully rebuilt their older organizations. The Farmers Union came into its own again and began to direct the attention of its members to the importance of collective buying.

To help the cause the Farmers Union Terminal Association, an old and established co-operative livestock marketing business, set aside $1,000 in 1927 to be used as the initial capital of a wholesale. By 1929 twenty co-operative associations owned shares in the Farmers Union Central Exchange. Within two years the number of local co-ops doubled and redoubled. In 1931 the wholesale volume was $900,000. It has grown steadily ever since.

This youngest and largest Farmers Union co-operative wholesale handles feed, fertilizer, general farm supplies, and petroleum products. With the increase in motorized farming, petroleum products have become the most important group of commodities sold through the organization.

Today the Farmers Co-operative and Educational

Union is almost unreservedly committed to the idea that consumers should co-operate for the purpose of rebuilding the distributive system. This is held necessary if the producers of agricultural products are ever to get justice in the market place. The triumph of this point of view was evident in 1937 when John Vesecky of Kansas was elected national president; H. G. Keeney of Nebraska, the vice-president; J. M. Graves of Oklahoma, secretary-treasurer; and Mrs. Gladys Talbott Edwards of North Dakota, National Junior Leader.

The youngest and largest national farmers' organization is the American Farm Bureau Federation. The first Farm Bureau was born in Broome County, New York, in 1913, a creature of the agricultural committee of the Binghamton Chamber of Commerce, the United States Department of Agriculture, and the Lackawanna Railroad. Its friends believe the Farm Bureau movement came into being to give the farmers a safe and sane solution to their difficulties. Its enemies claim that it is little better than a farmers' company union sponsored in the beginning by business interests which didn't want the farmers to be united in a single *farmers' union*.

The Farm Bureau became a national organization in 1919. Its original program was that of making the farmers more efficient producers. The watchword was: "Make two blades of grass grow where one grew before."

However, the rank and file of farmers have found that increased productive efficiency may in the end simply mean ruinous prices. Co-operative buying has come to receive a place in the organization's program. Recently the Farm Bureau has been giving increasing though somewhat grudging attention to the farmers' consumer interests. This is particularly true in Indiana, Ohio, and Pennsylvania.

The Indiana Farm Bureau Federation started a purchasing program in 1923. It sold fertilizer to its members through local business agents who operated much as similar officials had done in the early days of the Grange. The fertilizer was sold at reduced prices—a practice which brought on an all but ruinous price war with the fertilizer industry.

In 1924 Farm Bureau chain-stores were tried. Ten of these were established in what seemed strategic points. But the Indiana Farm Bureau did no better with the scheme than the Illinois Miners Union or the Nebraska Farmers Union. By 1925 losses totaling $12,000 had been incurred.

In order to keep the state Federation solvent its purchasing department was reorganized as the Indiana Farm Bureau Co-operative Association, an independent corporation. Mr. I. H. Hull was employed as general manager. The set-up was revamped and local co-operatives were established in nearly every county in the state. The chain-store set-up was completely liquidated. The state organization was made a wholesale, owned and controlled by 85 county units.

The new program is working. Its patrons include nearly one-half the farmers in the state. In 1937 the wholesale sold more than $6,000,000 worth of goods to county co-operatives. It handles tires, batteries, harness, feed, fertilizer, seeds, coal, baby chicks, farm machinery, electrical equipment, building material, paint, plumbing supplies, and petroleum products. It has developed its own hatcheries for producing disease-free chicks.

The Ohio Farm Bureau program of collective buying went through much the same evolution except that the process was slower. It began the distribution of commodities in 1920. In 1923 a subsidiary business organization was created—the Ohio Farm Bureau Service Company. Local distribution was carried on by farmers who acted as agents, by county Service Companies which were operated under the control and supervision of county Farm Bureau Federations, and a chain of stores owned and controlled by the state Service Company. This set-up survived for about a decade. Then general collapse set in. The centrally-owned stores didn't make their way; the local Service Companies got heavily involved in debt; membership in county Farm Bureau Federations melted away.

In 1934 a drastic reorganization program was put into effect. The Ohio Farm Bureau Service Company became the Ohio Farm Bureau Co-operative Association. Locally owned co-operative societies were established. Shares were purchased by the farmers in order to finance them. In most cases the county co-operatives were set up wholly independent of the control of Farm Bureau Federations. During the last four years rapid strides forward have been made. In 1936 the volume of the state wholesale was $6,750,000. The 78 county associations had a total volume of more than $11,000,000. In 1937 the wholesale volume was $8,450,000. Local associations enjoyed a like increase.

The Farm Bureau did not get off to an early start in Pennsylvania. The early twenties found the farmers of the state immune to the idea of starting another farm organization. But by 1934 there had developed a felt need for a co-operative program. A Farm Bureau organization was set up to provide this. A few local co-operatives were organized and a wholesale established at Harrisburg. There are nearly a score of local organizations at present. They are all flourishing and all well financed. In 1936 the sales of the wholesale were $511,887. In 1937 they were $950,000.

There are a number of other state Farm Bureaus having a program of collective purchasing for their members. Illinois has a large string of Farm Supply Companies which are semi-co-operative in character. They pay patronage refunds to those of their patrons who pay $15 per year dues to the Farm Bureau Federation. They pay eight per cent on share capital. However, the control is not democratic. Each Federation member in the territory served by a Supply Company is allowed a vote in the election of directors. But those who own preferred stock—and the capital was raised by the sale of preferred shares —have one vote per share. In business volume the Illinois Farm Bureau compares favorably with Ohio and Indiana.

Michigan and Iowa rank next in size and importance. In 1934 the wholesale volume of Farm Bureau Service Companies in both states had grown past $1,500,000. The Michigan group has worked in close connection with Indiana and Ohio in the distribution of fertilizer and petroleum products.

New York has the largest program of co-operative purchasing for farmers of any state in the Union. This development is unique in that it has three farmers' membership organizations all supporting a single project. The Farmers Union has never had much hold in the state. The Grange and the Farm Bureau are both powerful. The Dairymen's League has joined with them in promoting the Grange League Federation Co-operative Exchange—usually referred to as the G. L. F. It was established in 1920. The first two years were all but disastrous. Losses totaling $150,000 were incurred. But conservative management slowly redeemed the loss. The farmers had faith in co-operation and gave continued support. Today the G. L. F. serves 100,000 persons. Its annual turnover for 1937 was $60,000,000.

The Grange League Federaton has the distinction of being one co-operative in America to make the chain-store idea work. Much of its business is carried on through branch stores which are directly owned and controlled by the central organization whose headquarters are at Ithaca. Stores are established in communities where the farmers are willing to buy enough shares to finance them. The management is kept in touch with the will and desire of the customers through a democratically chosen management committee. Not all the business is done through branch stores, however. Many locally owned co-operatives use the G. L. F. for their wholesale.

The farmers' membership organizations have slowly come to realize the importance of consumer action and are advocating it. However, had there been no national farm organizations the farmers probably would have turned to it anyway. In certain areas the Granges, Farmers Unions, and Farm Bureaus, have given direction to the collective buying of farmers, but in others, co-operatives have grown because need spawned them.

In 1918 a small group of New England farmers decided their dollars weren't buying enough. They met at Springfield, Mass., and organized the Eastern States Farmers Exchange. They borrowed $30,000 to finance the organization. Today the Exchange has a membership of 82,500. Its volume for 1937 just missed being $20,000,000. The Exchange is not a wholesale, owned and controlled by local associations. It is a single unit. Its owners have direct membership in it. The distribution is carried on by local farmers who act as agents.

The farmers of Virginia had reason to complain about the prices and the quality of seed. So in 1922 they set up the Virginia Seed Service. Operations have since expanded to other commodities and the service to other states. It is now known as the Southern States Co-operative. Its headquarters are at Richmond. It is a little G. L. F. in form of organization and works closely with the larger co-operative after which it is patterned. In 1934 it fathered the Farmers Co-operative Exchange of North Carolina which is now a young but flourishing member of the farm co-operative family. The Southern States Co-operative had a volume of more than $5,000,000 in 1934. By 1937 the sales had grown to $10,264,000 per annum.

Inflated wartime prices of farm products started farmers buying motor cars and tractors in 1917 and 1918. Deflated post-war prices turned them to co-operation as a technique for buying motor fuel.

The first community to think of co-operative distribution of petroleum products was Cottonwood, Minnesota. There the co-op oil business got under

way in 1921. The same year saw the farmers of
Casco, Wisconsin, organizing America's second co-
operative oil association. The development stopped
there for three years. Then in 1924 came four more
associations in Minnesota. Another came into being
in 1925. In 1926 under the leadership of E. G.
Cort, once a county agricultural agent, thirteen co-
operatives formed the Midland Co-operative Oil
Association—our first wholesale for the co-operative
distribution of gasoline, kerosene, oil, and grease.
By 1930 the Midland was doing a business of
$600,000 per annum; 88 oil co-operatives were
operating in Minnesota and 50 in Wisconsin. In
1937 the Midland's volume was $3,600,000. In
1934 the co-ops stood third among the major oil companies in volume of business in Minnesota. They
moved to second place in 1935 and have held that
position since.

Minnesota pioneered in oil but the farmers of
other states soon caught the idea. Indiana's first
oil co-op came in 1926 at Crawfordsville. In 1929
the Farmers Union Central Exchange of St. Paul
got into the game. That same year a group of independent farmers' co-operatives around Kansas City
set up the Union Oil Company as a co-operative
wholesale. During the first year of operation 372
cars of kerosene and gasoline were handled. In the
year 1937-1938 the number was *6101*. In the meantime the Union Oil Company has become the Con-

sumers Co-operative Association with 420 affiliated local organizations."

Farmers working independent of national farm organizations also banded themselves together in the Texas panhandle and in the Pacific Northwest for the co-operative distribution of petroleum products. The result is the Consumers' Co-operatives Associated, of Amarillo and the Pacific Supply Co-operative of Walla Walla, Washington.

The petroleum business has been one of the great uniting factors in American co-operation. In 1930 the Ohio and Michigan Farm Bureau Service Companies and the Indiana Farm Bureau Co-operative Association decided to launch a joint venture in manufacturing. They formed the Farm Bureau Oil Company of Indianapolis and invested $40,000 in a blending plant for the manufacture of oils and greases. The venture paid for itself out of earnings in fourteen months. By 1935 its net worth had grown to $135,000. When the Pennsylvania Farm Bureau Co-operative was formed, it joined the Farm Bureau Oil Company. In 1936 G. L. F., the Southern States Co-operatives, the Farmers Co-operative Exchange, and the Maryland Farm Bureau asked to get into the picture. The Farm Bureau Oil Company was reorganized as the United Co-operatives, Inc. A new plant was built in 1937 to take care of the growing demand for its products.

In February, 1933, eight co-operative wholesales

interested in motor fuels and oils formed a buying pool called National Co-operatives. The organization was set up in Chicago with the following groups represented: the Midland, the Farmers Union Central Exchange, the Union Oil Company (Co-operative), the Consumers' Co-operatives Associated, the Central Co-operative Wholesale, and the three groups in the Farm Bureau Oil Company. At the time of its organization 577 local co-operatives were involved. Their total membership was 500,000—mostly farmers. In 1934 the Pacific Supply Co-operative was added to the list. In 1936 the reorganization of the Farm Bureau Oil Company brought in the new groups forming United Co-operatives.

The first year's purchases of National Co-operatives included 14,000 cars of gasoline, 3,500,000 gallons of lubricating oil and 2,500,000 pounds of grease. Today, paint, electrical equipment, and farm machinery are also being handled.

A third large section of the co-operative farm supply business is being carried on by organizations whose original and primary purpose is to get the farmers more for what they produce—the marketing associations. These collective bargaining agencies date back to the nineteenth century. In 1892 farmers around Rockwell, Iowa, decided to market their own grain through a co-operative elevator. This decision led to a seven years' war with those who were in the grain business. In the end the organization won the right to live and the co-operative elevator movement became a permanent part of American agriculture.

It was carried forward during the first two decades of the present century by both the Farmers Union and the Equity Union, a farmers' membership organization which also began in 1902 but has since practically disappeared. The Equity Union was successful, however, in establishing a number of co-operative elevators, livestock marketing associations, and creameries. It was a factor in getting farmers interested in the ownership of marketing machinery and has helped many an independent farmers' elevator get under way.

But strange as it may seem many of the elevators, set up to market grain, have developed a consumer business which is greater than the marketing operations. They sell feed, fertilizer, twine, spray materials, coal, and other farm supplies, and pay patronage dividends to those who purchase them. Some have even entered the petroleum and fuel business. Groups of such elevators have set up wholesale marketing and purchasing organizations—selling grain and buying supplies. Two of the largest of these are the Missouri Farmers Association and the Ohio Farmers Grain and Supply Association. The Missouri organization has headquarters in Kansas City. It operates a feed mill at Springfield and an oil association at Columbia. In 1934 its mill turned out $1,861,000 worth of products. In 1937 the gross volume had grown to $4,396,765. The net profit on milling alone was $124,000.

The Ohio organization is located at Fostoria. The state has about 225 co-operative elevators which do a supply business of around $9,000,000 per year. The Fostoria Grain and Supply Co-operative acts as wholesale for them.

Altogether there are over 6,000 local farmers' elevators in America, most of which carry on joint marketing and purchasing business.

But it is not just the co-op elevators which have been busy at this sort of thing. Fruit, cotton, poultry, and dairy marketing associations are doing it. According to government statistics the largest of these are Land of Lakes Creameries of Minneapolis, California Fruit Exchange of Sacramento, Fruit Growers Supply Company of Los Angeles, Utah Poultry Producers Co-operative Association of Salt Lake City, Washington Co-operative Egg and Poultry Association of Seattle, Poultrymen's Co-operative Association of Southern California at Los Angeles.

The American farmer is in revolt. He has become alarmed at the foreclosures which are slowly depriving him of ownership of his lands. He resents the fact that he gets only 10% of the nation's income although farmers and their families compose 25% of the population.

In the past his revolt has expressed itself in a

variety of ways. In some areas he started marketing co-operatives, in some he organized himself politically, thinking that a friendly government would solve his difficulties. Now and again a violent strike would be launched to procure better prices for farm products.

Slowly, however, the emphasis passes to action as consumers. It has been the program which has served best, grown the fastest, accomplished most in dollar and cents results, and given control of the greatest amount of economic machinery.

Within recent years the farm supply co-operatives have been invading the field of processing and manufacturing. There are now four co-operative oil-blending plants in America. They are owned and operated by the Midland Co-operative Wholesale, the Farmers Union Central Exchange, the Consumers Co-operative Association, and United Co-operatives. The G. L. F. manufactures most of its own feed in mills with a capacity of 75 cars per day. The Eastern States Exchange has mills capable of producing 50 cars every 24 hours. In addition it owns and operates two fertilizer plants. The Ohio Farmers Grain and Supply Association makes its own fertilizers. The Fruit Growers Supply Company has a lumber yard with a capacity of 50,000,000 feet. It turns out a vast supply of boxes, baskets, and other fruit containers each year. During 1938 the Farm Bureau Co-operatives of Ohio and the G. L. F.

purchased fertilizer plants of their own and put them into operation. Indiana co-operatives are in the process of building a fertilizer plant at Indianapolis. They already own and operate one of the most modern seed cleaning establishments in the country. The Southern States Co-operative owns three fertilizer plants with a combined capacity of 172,000 tons per year, and three feed mills capable of producing 85 cars of feed per day.

CHAPTER X

An Old Controversy Rages

THE FARMERS STARTED co-operatives because economic necessity drove them to it. They were motivated by no particular idealism; had no clear conception of creating a new economic system. They were in trouble, and began co-operative purchasing as a means of helping themselves. Serious economic difficulty came to agricultural America at the close of the World War. Intense interest in co-operatives began at the same time. There was nothing accidental about this. Co-operation has always thrived on adversity.

In the beginning the agricultural co-operator looked upon his business enterprise primarily as a money-saving device. It made it possible for him to stretch the buying power of his dollar. His major hopes for solving economic difficulties were focused at another point—he wanted more for what he had to sell. His chief interest was in increasing the returns from the labor which he marketed indirectly, by selling the things which his work produced. He thought of his difficulties primarily as producer problems. Organization of his consumer interest was incidental—in his thinking—to the solving of his other perplexities.

He was encouraged to think of himself as a producer and not as a consumer by his occupational federations—whether Grange, Farmers Union, or Farm Bureau. These organizations reflected his thinking. They also served to perpetuate the direction and terms of his thought. The Farmers Union has persistently hammered at the need of a strong *class* organization. The Farm Bureau has shied at the curt word *class* but encouraged producer-mindedness by tying itself to the county-agent system which provided technical advisors to teach the farmer how to increase production. Both organizations kept attention riveted on his producer problems, telling him that their solution would bring him the security he desired. It was inevitable that when consumer organizations were established they should be regarded simply as aids to the solving of occupational problems.

The motives of the American farmer in forming purchasing organizations were basically the same as that of the Rochdale Pioneers. In the beginning, they saw in their store simply a means to an end—the end being to secure ownership of the factories and machines which they made productive by their labor. Ownership would give them adequate rewards for their work, and freedom from the insecurity of owning no property. The farmers' organizations have been dominated by men whose thinking was very similar to that of the Christian Socialists who exalted the interest of producers to the very end.

Within the ranks of agricultural co-operators a battle is raging much like that which shook the English co-operative movement for almost half a century. The old question as to whether or not consumer or producer interest is the most important is very much alive today.

The controversy has hardly reached the farm marketing associations which carry on a consumer business for their members. Their focal point of interest is still in the marketing field. Their primary purpose is to get producers more for their products. They purchase supplies for members in order to cut the costs of production for them. Usually they handle no general consumer goods. A very few elevators handle coal and gasoline but these items are relatively unimportant side lines. Naturally, the leadership of these marketing associations has no sense of identity with the world-wide consumers' movement. They are not particularly hostile to it but are almost wholly indifferent to it.

Those who formulate the philosophy for the marketing groups are essential followers of Robert Owen. They believe with him that producers must be organized in order that they may secure for themselves the full returns from their productive effort. Like him they regard co-operative purchasing as an incidental feature of the more important producer program.

Within the American Farm Bureau Federation the struggle is very much alive today. Its national leadership is almost wholly engrossed with the question of how to increase the farmer's share of the national income. It has consistently supported the government in the AAA program—including all proposals for creating an artificial scarcity through limiting production. It does not frown on economic co-operation but believes in it for farmers and for farmers only. It sees no virtue in the consumer approach to the problems of rural people. It looks with disfavor on the general consumers' co-operative movement—fearing that it will compromise the interests of farmers. Their point of view is not dissimilar from that of the Christian Socialist of nineteenth century England who had such holy fear that the consumers' co-operatives were encroaching on the sacred rights of producers.

Some of the state Farm Bureau Federations follow the national leaders of the organization. A significant minority do not. The Indiana, Ohio, and Pennsylvania groups are manifesting a growing interest in general consumer action. They have officially endorsed the efforts of city dwellers to establish co-operatives for themselves. Officers of Indiana's Farm Bureau gave material aid to Indianapolis' first co-operatively owned filling station

—investing money and time in an effort to interest urban people in the co-operative method of distributing petroleum products.

The leaders of the Ohio Farm Bureau are doing much to get the farmers of that state to consider themselves consumers. There is a growing acceptance of the position of Adam Smith that consumption is the sole end and purpose of all production and that the interest of the producer is secondary to that of the consumer. This does not mean that the Ohio Farm Bureau is not doing all within its power to get agricultural producers a fairer share of the national income. It does mean that it sees no escape from the present economic chaos without consumer co-operative ownership of the means of production and distribution. The Pennsylvania leadership has a like point of view.

The Farmers Union and the Indiana, Ohio, and Pennsylvania Farm Bureaus are in essential agreement. The Farmers Union press is filled with news about consumer co-operatives. The educational program of the Union includes consumers' co-operation. The wholesale facilities are put freely at the disposal of urban as well as rural co-operatives. Of the three national farm organizations it has most completely and wholeheartedly endorsed the consumers' co-operative approach to present-day economic problems.

But while all this is true, the Farmers Union and

the liberal element in the Farm Bureau still have some reservations about forgetting occupational differences in co-operative organizations. Both groups practice a co-operative dualism. They encourage and abet the general consumers' movement but at the same time keep occupational barriers around the co-operatives which they have sponsored. The membership in the co-operative associations of the Farm Bureau and Farmers Union is nearly always limited to "producers of agricultural products." Others are permitted to buy, but as yet are not accepted as fellow consumers with equal rights and privileges.

The more recently organized independent co-operatives, which came into being without a farmers' organization acting as mid-wife and nurse for them, have naturally manifested the least interest in producer economic activities and gone the farthest in asserting the primary importance of the consumer approach to our present puzzling problems. They have no objections to producers' marketing associations. In fact they heartily favor them as a means of increasing the income of farmers.

And they believe in farmers' class organizations to protect agricultural interests in the halls of government. But they also believe that there is no security for the rural population apart from the well-being of the urban people; they regard our basic economic problems as things which concern the people as a whole. They see consumers' co-operation as the battle-line of all exploited, disinherited people against want and insecurity. They urge the farmer to join co-operatives not primarily for the purpose of furthering his interests as a producer but to enrich his life as a consumer and a human being. They point out that the fundamental reason for farmers wanting more for what they sell is to give greater access to the great store of consumer goods which our industrial machinery is capable of producing. The basic desire is for more things to consume. The real concern is for a better standard of living.

These independent co-operative groups were started by farmers, today they are largely supported by farmers, but they have little interest in occupational differences. They draw no lines between people because they happen to make their living at different kinds of work. The *Midland Co-operator*, official organ of the Midland wholesale and its affiliates, boldly carries this statement of purpose: "devoted to building the consumers' co-operative movement." Though started by farm people, the Midland is giving encouragement to persons of all occupations to organize themselves as consumers—particularly for the distribution of petroleum products. The Consumers Co-operative Association of Kansas City—once the Union Oil Company—is working along similar lines. It is now encouraging both filling stations and stores handling groceries and household necessities. The change in name is a reflection of a consciousness of larger purposes.

The drift within the farmers' co-operative movement is toward the point of view dominant in these independent groups. Certain straws point the direction. One indicator is the increasing number of farmers' purchasing associations which are affiliating with the Co-operative League—which has always insisted that the consumer interest of men and women was a solvent for the barriers which divided them as producers. The first wholesale to take this step was the Grange organization of Seattle. It became a League member in 1929. The Midland followed in 1930.

Four years later the directors of National Co-operatives voted to accept membership with the older educational federation. This brought within the scope of the League influence over six hundred local co-operative associations. As other wholesales have joined the National this number has been greatly increased. This affiliation does not mean that all the members of the local societies involved, or even all the officials of the wholesales, are thinking of their business institutions as servants of all the people. It does mean that the directors of National Co-operatives and the groups which are a part of it are sufficiently interested in the promotion of a general consumers' movement to want to have fellowship with the League which is working toward that end.

A second pointer is the frequency with which farmers' organizations carry news about urban co-operatives in their official publications: the Oklahoma and Nebraska *Union Farmer*, the northwest's *Farmers Union Herald*, the Indiana Farm Bureau's *Hoosier Farmer*, the *Ohio Farm Bureau News*, the *Co-operative Review* of the Pennsylvania Farm Bureau are all carrying stories of consumers' co-operative achievements—urban and rural.

In England, time and circumstances greatly assisted John T. W. Mitchell and his disciples in their struggle with the Christian Socialists. In America, practical, perhaps much more than theoretical considerations are leading farmers in the same direction.

The large oil companies have not taken the increasing competition of co-operatives lying down. They have not been asleep to the fact that they have lost fourteen per cent of the nation's tank wagon business. Because the oil associations have been so largely farmer-owned the capitalistic distributors of petroleum products have slashed prices in territories served by co-operatives operating tank trucks. In many cases gasoline is sold off the truck for 3½ and 4 cents less than it is through filling stations. The co-ops have had to meet these price cuts. In many cases profits have all but disappeared. The oil companies with a large urban business can afford to fight the farmers' co-operatives by price-cutting so long as they have the profits from the filling-station trade to keep them going. In this struggle the farmers are beginning to see the need of allies. In self-defense they are being forced to think in more inclusive terms. Self-preservation is a first law of life for economic as well as biological organisms. Rural co-operators know they must get into the filling-station business if the wide margins of profit in that field are to flow through co-operative channels. They also know that exclusively farmer-owned filling stations can never command the loyal support of those who live in villages, towns, and cities. They are beginning to see that they need all the help they can get from urban people.

Also the grocery men, coal, lumber, and feed dealers are taking up the fight against co-operatives. This opposition bids fair to bring about a unity of thought and action which theorizing alone could never do.

Then, too, trends within agriculture itself fight for the consumer-minded. There was a time when each American farm was a nearly self-sufficient economic unit. The food and clothing of the farm family came off the land. Home spinning, weaving, and sewing provided clothing. Home gardening, canning, butchering, and baking provided the food. Not many of the farmer's dollars found their way into the clothing or grocery store. But now wool, flax, and cotton are all cash crops. They are sold to processors from which the farm family secures clothing. Home production of foodstuffs likewise slowly disappears. Home baked bread is becoming as rare on rural tables as it is on urban. In certain areas home butchering is a thing of the past. Creamery butter and oleomargarine certainly are not rarities at "country dinners." More and more of the farmer's income is spent for food. The grocery bill is an increasingly important item in his budget.

This trend naturally focuses attention on the possibility of co-operative purchasing of food. The farmers who have done so well with motor fuel and general agricultural supplies are not likely to let food and clothing go permanently neglected. There is only one way to think of organizing a co-operative food or clothing store—that is on the basis of general consumer ownership. Even the most decidedly producer-minded agriculturist can't get very enthusiastic about organizing a special class of co-operative grocery stores to serve the producers of farm products.

The increasing specialization of agriculture is making it more difficult to maintain the unity of farmers in an occupational fraternity. The corn farmer sells his corn to the cotton and dairy farmer. The cotton farmer produces the raw material for the clothing of all other types of farmers. The wheat farmer is rapidly becoming a specialist, producing for the entire population. High prices for one class of farmers often means reduced purchasing power for another class. The producer interest of one class of farmers is very often in essential conflict with the producer interest of another. The cleavages between classes of farm producers are just as great as the cleavage between the farmer as a producer and the city laborer as a producer. This important fact gnaws at the heart of the farmer's occupational class consciousness. As farmers grow increasingly dependent upon others for the goods and services they use, as geographic division of labor destroys self-sufficiency, agricultural producers must turn to consumers' co-operation in their search for a common approach to their economic problems.

In America as elsewhere, time, coupled with inevitable trends within agriculture itself, will have much to do with settling a controversy which is almost as ancient as the co-operative movement itself. Rural America is coming of age economically.

CHAPTER XI

The City Follows Suit

IT MAY BE THAT THE long awaited day of the consumers' co-operative movement is at hand in America. Certainly there is a growing concern with general consumer problems and an increasing interest in co-operatives.

The best sellers of the last few years have been books dealing with consumer problems. Those who buy the food and clothing for American households eagerly read anything which promises them help in the matter of spending money. They want to know the relative merits of various products and brands. Literature debunking advertising is read with almost malicious glee. Consumers want more facts and less fiction about the goods they use.

Home Demonstration Agents of the Agricultural Extension Service find rural women eager to become intelligent purchasers. 4-H clubs, domestic science departments of high schools and colleges are seeking to create a generation of homekeepers who will be scientific choosers in the market place.

Public and private educational institutions are beginning to teach courses on Consumer Problems.

This represents a new emphasis. In the immediate past education has been largely engrossed with technical training. The laboratories and experimental stations of colleges and universities have been second only to the stadiums in size and importance. Young men and women have been trained for efficient production. Education has been dedicated to occupational preparation. But there is a growing awareness that men and women are fundamentally consumers. The ability to use intelligently consumer goods is something which graces life long after the individual's productive days are over.

These things are straws in the wind. Americans are coming into consumer self-consciousness. To be sure the biggest consumer problem of the average person is getting goods to consume. No consumer training is fundamental which does not attempt to give the masses of men a way by which they can tap for themselves the world's great resources of wealth.

But the fundamentals are not being neglected. The demand for information about the co-operative way of carrying on business was never so great. Presses are busy printing pamphlets and books on the subject. Libraries which for years were barren of co-operative literature have recently purchased volumes of it in response to growing demand.

American labor is showing signs of a revival of its interest in consumer action. It is apparently the one thing upon which the followers of William L. Green and the disciples of John L. Lewis can agree. Sobering events of the closing months of 1937 and the first weeks of 1938 have helped the revival. Labor has been on an organizational spree. Unionism has been the vogue. The right to bargain collectively for wages and hours has been sought after and fought for. But labor does not have security even when unionized unless there are jobs to be had. The lengthening relief rolls of 1937 and 1938 have made it clear that unions are not enough. There must be some way of insuring adequate distribution of goods, responsive to America's ability to consume. The American Federation of Labor, the United Rubber Workers, the Steel Workers Organizing Committee, are urging the organization of co-operatives. Homer Martin, of the United Automobile Workers, is preaching a like doctrine to that turbulent union.

This is not the first time labor has shown interest in consumer action. The Protective Union movement was the child of a labor union. The Knights of Labor heartily endorsed consumers' co-operation. The wave of societies which emerged and died during the second decade of the present century had generous labor support. But for the past fifteen years the American union laborer has been almost wholly interested in getting higher wages and shorter hours. He had no interest in organizing himself as a consumer. During the boom days before

1929 he thought he was secure. Now he knows better. He is beginning to think about consumer protection.

The general interest in co-operatives is being reflected in the increasing business volume of old societies and the number of new ones being organized. Urbanites are following in the footsteps of their country cousins. Co-operative stores and filling stations are no longer found only in hamlets and county seat towns. In the larger population centers they are breaking out like measles on a ten year old.

In 1929 consumers' co-operation seemed dead in California. Only three societies were left out of the once proud movement in that state. But the ravages of the depression are changing the picture. Her people tried to elect Upton Sinclair governor because he promised "to end poverty in California." Failing in that they have gone back to the less spectacular co-operative method of solving their problems. The state has a new group of co-operative societies. They have organized themselves into two educational federations: the Co-operative Education Association of Los Angeles, and the Northern California Co-operative Council of Oakland. In both northern and southern California, co-operative stores are buying together in federations which may soon become co-operative wholesales.

At the beginning of the depression the Central States Co-operative League—the Illinois survival of the events of the early twenties—was a dying institution. Its societies were failing one at a time. League officials whistled to keep up their courage. The offices were at Bloomington, Illinois—the center of an increasing co-operative desert. The League was supposed to serve southern Michigan, Illinois, Indiana, and Ohio. But it would never have survived had it not been for the Finnish and Bohemian co-operators of Dillonvale and Cleveland, Ohio, Chicago and Waukegan, Illinois.

Today the League pulsates with life. New societies, organized by teachers, office-workers, preachers, lawyers, and club women began to appear around Chicago, Detroit, Cincinnati, Cleveland. The offices are now in Chicago. In 1936 a small wholesale was started. In 1937 it served 60 member societies to which it made sales totaling $107,000. Gary and Indianapolis, Indiana; Columbus, Cincinnati, and Cleveland, Ohio; Flint, Ann Arbor, and Detroit, Michigan; Chicago and the cities which nest about it, all boast newly established stores and filling stations. In southern Michigan and around Cincinnati local educational federations have been set up to help make the movement effective in those areas.

On the east coast like events are taking place. In 1925 the Eastern States Co-operative League was established to assist the national League in promoting co-operation on the northern half of the Atlantic seaboard. This venture received its best support from the Finlanders of Massachusetts and a handful of large societies in New York City and Brooklyn. In 1937 New York had three co-operative housing societies with a total membership of 1,031 families. Consumers Co-operative Services, which operates a chain of cafeterias, had 4,500 members; the Co-operative Trading Association of Brooklyn 2,400. There was a sprinkling of other small fry which brought the total number of League member societies to 49. The Eastern Co-operative Wholesale of New York was established in 1929 with 7 affiliates. From 1935 to 1937 its business volume increased from $203,720 to $533,134. In 1935 it had 11 affiliated societies. By May 1938 this figure had grown to 97.

Boston and Philadelphia have active co-operative groups operating new business enterprises. The nation's capital has two growing societies. Pittsburgh and its environs boasts a revival of interest in consumers' co-operation.

In the Old Northwest the Midland wholesale of Minneapolis and the Central Wholesale at Superior are serving an ever-increasing number of urban societies. The Midland recently established a branch warehouse at Milwaukee in order to better serve the co-operatively owned filling stations of Wisconsin. Madison, Kenosha, Racine, and Milwaukee all have rapidly growing young co-ops. Wisconsin law requires that public educational institutions teach the principles and practices of consumers' co-operation.

Minnesota is the nation's greatest co-operative state. The high percentage of north Europeans among her people has been a factor in the growth of consumer societies. Minneapolis and St. Paul have strong co-operatives serving an expanding host of people.

Much good for the cause has been done by the Northern States Co-operative League with headquarters in Minneapolis. In the beginning its support came largely from Finnish organizations. It has consistently striven to help all interested groups without regard to their nationality. In 1936 it had 475 member societies representing 167,000 families. The majority of these were rural but the percentage from the cities steadily increases. The co-operators of this area are generally less concerned with the occupational differences of men and women than those of some other sections. The doors of most of the co-operatives are open to all who wish to identify themselves with the movement. No lines are drawn between country folks and city dwellers.

In the great western water-shed of the Mississippi river the Consumers Co-operative Association of North Kansas City is a rallying center for both urban and rural societies. Within the past five years city groups have come to play a much more important role in its affairs. Denver, Colorado; Des

Moines, Iowa; St. Louis, and Columbia, Missouri; the two Kansas Cities; Manhattan and Emporia, Kansas; Enid, Oklahoma, are all centers of new developments.

Enid now has a wholesale established June 1, 1936. It is called Oklahoma Co-operatives, Inc. It works in close connection with the Association at North Kansas City using the older organization as a source of supply. It now serves 30 societies. In 1937 it handled over 2,000,000 gallons of motor fuel.

In the Pacific Northwest, the Grange Wholesale and the Pacific Supply Co-operative feel the impact of growing urban movements. The petroleum volume of the latter organization increased 20 per cent in 1937. It routed over 13,000,000 gallons of petroleum products to consumer-owned stations. It is seriously considering expansion into the grocery business.

Add the growth of urban co-operatives to the increasing strength of the rural societies and the evidence is clear that American consumers are not content to stop without trying to solve the fundamental problem of the average consumer—how to get goods to consume.

The co-operatives are not only increasing in numbers but they are operating in a widening variety of fields. Mention has already been made of the large quantities of farm supplies purchased by co-operating farmers. There are a host of organizations selling petroleum products through filling stations and off tank trucks. The grocery store has always been a favorite co-operative enterprise. In a few places consumers own their own dairies. The largest single society in America is the Franklin Co-operative Creamery of Minneapolis which has handled $45,-000,000 worth of milk products since its organization in 1921. The Co-operative Trading Company of Waukegan operates 26 milk routes.

At Dillonvale, Ohio, we have America's first consumer-owned packing plant. This was built in 1936 by the New Co-operative Company to supply its stores with fresh meats and sausages.

The people of a number of communities in Minnesota and Iowa have grown weary of high funeral costs and have set up societies to provide this service for themselves. The first of the Iowa associations was established at George in 1927. The state now has nine others. The total membership is 12,000 families. Minnesota has nearly a score of like associations. In 1936 there were 42 in the whole country serving 27,000 members.

Many rural sections have co-operative telephone companies which have been in operation almost from the beginning of the famed "party line." Within the last two years, through the help of the New Deal's Rural Electrification Administration, a large number of co-operative electric lines have been built. The first of these was in Boone County, Indiana. Ohio alone has projects in operation which serve 15,000 farms.

In New York City the Amalgamated Clothing Workers have made a splendid showing with co-operative apartment houses. Eight hundred sixty families are organized in two societies: the Amalgamated Housing Corporation and Amalgamated Dwellings. In connection with their housing projects they operate grocery stores, laundry service, a co-operative school bus service, and a children's summer camp.

Almost from their beginning in America co-operatives have sold clothing. Within the last few months some of the large farm co-operatives have begun handling dress as well as work clothes. Specially constructed trucks carrying the merchandise make periodic calls into the territories served. Temporary displays are set up and the consumers invited to come and inspect the wares.

In areas into which electric lines have been recently built, the co-operative distribution of electrical goods has developed. National Co-operatives now provides its member societies with a complete line of refrigerators, radios, washing machines, and vacuum cleaners.

Indiana has a few co-operatively owned lumber yards. Hardware stores are by no means rare.

In the old Northwest co-operative garages, operated in connection with filling stations, are maintained. In some cases these garages not only provide a repair service, they merchandise automobiles as well.

America has one society engaged entirely in the publishing business. It is the Co-operative Publishing Association of Superior, Wisconsin. It maintains a weekly paper called the *Co-operative Builder* and sells books, pamphlets, and similar merchandise to its members. The Co-operative Book Club, a national organization, located at 118 East 28th Street, New York, supplies individuals' book needs and maintains a wholesale book service for co-operatives, public libraries and institutions.

Only recently the United States Bureau of Labor statistics published its findings on the status of the American co-operative movement in 1936. It found a total of 3,600 societies handling consumer goods. The membership was 677,000 and the annual business volume $182,685,000. 2,400 were store societies, having 330,500 members and a volume totaling $107,250,000 per annum; 1,150 were oil associations with 325,000 members. Their sales totaled $69,985,000. Other distributive societies were 50 in number. They had 22,250 members and sales totaling $5,450,000. Of the 3,600 associations handling consumer goods 1,173 were serving farm families almost exclusively. The combined membership of these rural organizations was 303,000 families; their annual volume $111,998,641.

The above figures do not include an additional

1,000 associations specializing in farm supplies. Organizations of this type have 646,000 members and annual sales of $142,000,000. Nor does it include the nation's 3,728 co-operative telephone associations serving 330,000 families, or the 259 electric supply co-operatives which provide current for 161,000 farm homes.

Co-operative Insurance is a growing part of the movement. The Farm Bureau Mutual Insurance Company of Columbus, Ohio, serves eight states and is the fifth largest mutual automobile casualty company in the United States. The Workmen's Mutual Fire Insurance Society of New York has an honorable history running over half a century. The Farmers Union and the Grange both carry on ambitious insurance programs for their members. There are a great many small co-operative fire-insurance companies operating among farmers. The Northern States Co-operative League operates a co-operative life insurance company.

Consumers are not only organizing themselves in increasing numbers in America, they are providing themselves with an expanding variety of services. The list of goods and services which can be purchased co-operatively grows with the size and power of the movement. Americans are learning that there are few things important for good living which cannot be distributed through channels owned by consumers themselves.

CHAPTER XII

Strength and Weakness

RECENT YEARS in America's co-operative history have been characterized by unprecedented growth. Since 1934 many of the larger wholesales have had annual increases in business volume ranging from 20 to 50 per cent. While capitalistic business has wallowed in the doldrums, co-operatives have sold more goods, expanded services, and employed an increasing army of people.

However, rapidity of growth is not of necessity an indication of strength or permanency. There have been periods of swift expansion in the past. The early Grange movement grew by leaps and bounds. Co-operatives were being established about as fast in 1918 and 1919 as they are now, but the death rate from 1920 to 1923 was equal to the growth rate of the boom period. Only a foolish or uninformed optimist would accept the fact of rapid expansion as certain evidence that an ever greater portion of American business will flow through co-operative channels in the future.

An unguided spirit of expansionism is in itself dangerous. Unless controlled by the discipline of economic facts and the stern finality of balance sheets it is heady wine for a young co-operative movement. A co-operative that does not grow eventually dies, but one which expands too fast is just as certain to come to an untimely end. Over-expansion is one of the threats against the permanency of many American co-operatives.

The situation in one section of the farm movement is a case in point. During 1933, 1934, and 1935 one of the state branches of a farmers' organization promoted a string of local co-operative societies and established a wholesale to serve the territory with petroleum products and general farm supplies. Most of the local associations were started with inadequate capital. General farm conditions were bad and it was hard to sell enough shares to properly finance them. But in spite of this handicap reasonable initial success was achieved. As the co-operatives grew the eagerness of the leaders of the development increased. They began to urge local boards of directors to push new items. Electrical appliances, farm machinery, clothing, and even groceries were taken on. Before accumulated profits relieved the financial situation for one set of services new ones were added. Increased inventories have created great strain for capital structures. Lack of resources have made it hard to carry the necessary overhead involved in proper merchandising of such items as tractors, farm tools, electric refrigerators, and radios.

The situation has been further complicated by

refusal to adopt the Rochdale practice of cash trading. The statement, "Farmers must have credit," has been interpreted to mean, "co-operatives must extend credit to farmers." The state organization has given local boards of directors no encouragement to go on a cash basis. Managers were given no training in handling the perplexities involved in credit control.

Naturally, this has created a thoroughly unhealthy condition. There is a general awakening to its dangers and efforts being made at reform but it is not yet time to assume these co-operatives will be permanent parts of the American movement.

Urban co-operators are subject to the same disease. In 1937 representatives from groups interested in city grocery stores met in Columbus, Ohio, to discuss their common problems. They spent nearly a day talking about the possibility of establishing a wholesale in that city—ignoring the fact that there were only a handful of local stores in operation in the state and few of them had money to invest in the capital stock of a wholesale. The co-operators of another American city actually launched a wholesale before they had organized a single successful local store to buy from it. This eagerness for a wholesale is one of the most common types of over-expansionism.

It also takes the form of starting under-financed stores. In one Illinois city a group of enthusiasts wanted to get into business shortly after they heard about co-operatives. They raised a few hundred dollars, bought out a small merchant, and started into business for themselves. For a time it seemed that membership loyalty would overcome the handicap of inadequate capital. But an unforeseen accident involved the society in expensive litigation. There were no reserves to take care of such an emergency. The store had to close its doors. The co-operative movement would have been further ahead in that city if there had been less haste.

The overeagerness of enthusiasts undoubtedly will continue to doom other newly established societies to an early death.

Overlapping of territory is a weakness of the co-operative wholesale structure of the country. It is not likely to be fatal either to established wholesales or to local societies but it does make for duplication of services and lack of co-ordination. The state of Washington has both the Grange Co-operative Wholesale and the Pacific Supply Co-operative. The territory served by the Consumers Co-operative Association overlaps with that of the Farmers Union Jobbing Association of Kansas, the Farmers Union Exchange of Nebraska, and the Missouri Farmers Association. In Minnesota, the Midland Co-operative Wholesale and the Farmers Union Central Exchange are located within a few miles of each other. The territory served by the Midland's Milwaukee branch and the Central Co-operative Wholesale of Superior overlap. In Ohio some County Farm Bureau Co-operatives and farmers' elevators buying through the Fostoria Grain and Supply Co-operative operate in competition with each other. To further complicate the picture the Ohio State Grange sells fertilizer, twine, paint, and oil through local business agents. The Pennsylvania Farm Bureau co-operatives and Eastern States Farmers Exchange compete in portions of Pennsylvania. In Oklahoma there are both a Farmers Union state exchange and the newly created Oklahoma Co-operatives, Inc.

A part of this situation is the result of American geography. The United States is as large as Europe. There is a very definite limit to the amount of territory which a wholesale house can serve profitably. As co-operatives were established in regions not being served by existing wholesales new ones naturally came into being. In the course of time there was inevitable overlapping at the fringes. Only careful advance planning could have prevented it.

Some of the present duplication has its roots in past commodity specialization. For instance, the first co-operatives handling petroleum products were new organizations set up originally for the marketing of a single group of commodities. At the time the Midland wholesale was established the Central Co-operative Wholesale was not interested in petroleum products. Its societies were almost exclusively engaged in the grocery business. It was perfectly natural for the oil associations to create a separate wholesale to provide themselves with gasoline, kerosene, oil, and grease. Since that time the societies affiliated with the Central wholesale have started handling petroleum products and the Midland affiliates have become interested in groceries and farm supplies. Societies in each group continue to look to the organization from which they have been habitually buying to supply them with the new commodities as their distribution is undertaken.

When the Consumers Co-operative Association was first formed it was called the Union Oil Company. Its original purpose was to market one type of merchandise. The Farmers Union wholesales of the area were not then paying much attention to the gasoline and oil business. Since then the Farmers Union wholesales have become interested in petroleum, and the oil co-ops in expanding their services into other lines.

But neither an outgrown commodity specialization nor geography can wholly account for all the overlapping. No small part of it is due to continued domination by sponsoring organizations. This is particularly true of those set up by state Granges, Farm Bureaus, and Farmers Unions. These groups started co-operatives as a part of their general program for helping farmers solve their problems. Loyalty to the idea of co-operation implied loyalty to the sponsoring organization and its total program. Devotion to the total program meant faithful support of business enterprises. Neither leaders nor rank and file farmers ever thought of separating the two. The co-operative staffs worked freely and faithfully to promote membership in the farm organization which sponsored them. In many cases it became customary to simply deduct annual dues from patronage dividends. This greatly simplified the matter of collecting these regular contributions to state and national treasuries. The co-operative program, where successful, inevitably enhanced the prestige and power of the so-called *parent* body. Farmers Union, Grange, and Farm Bureau officials would have to be idealists of the purest sort, if they were not more eager to see co-operatives established which bear the label of their organization than they are to see independent societies supplying their members with goods.

Motives of this kind easily account for the overlapping of Grange, Farm Bureau, and independent co-operative purchasing in Ohio; for the setting up of the Farmers Union Exchange almost next door to the Midland wholesale.

The labeling of co-operatives with the name of a sponsoring group makes for duplication in another way. There are always those persons who do not endorse the total program of the parent body, who for a host of reasons have no interest in the particular point of view of an occupational class organization. In areas where labeled co-operatives have been established, these people are faced with the choice of supporting a co-operative bearing a name that either arouses antagonism or is without significance for them, establishing an independent unlabeled society, or buying through the usual non-co-operative sources. Not infrequently they choose the second alternative. That was the choice in Oklahoma and the Oklahoma Co-operatives came into being right under the nose of a Farmers Union state exchange.

The American co-operative movement will not reach its full stature until its leaders have found a way of eliminating from the wholesale structure this lack of co-ordination.

But weighing against the weaknesses of expansionism and overlapping are certain factors making for their correction. One of these is the extensive development of adult education among co-operative societies. For a number of years the burden of educational work was largely carried on by the national and district Leagues. Today these organizations become increasingly supervisory and advisory in character while the work of teaching the principles and practices of co-operation is being carried on by wholesales, local societies, and small regional councils such as the Chicago Co-operative Union and the Cincinnati Co-operative League. And this is all to the good. It would be utterly impossible for the district and national Leagues to keep up with the present demand for information without increasing help from local groups.

Today there is hardly a co-operative wholesale in the national League which does not have an educational department. Certain sections of the farm organizations are doing yeoman service in this field. They are including co-operative education in their program, developing a growing number of study groups, conferences, and summer camps in which people are being taught how to operate their own business enterprises. Managers, directors, employees, co-operative shareholders, and young people attend and achieve a better understanding of their functions in the co-operative movement.

This makes for a healthy attitude of self-criticism, creates the ability to recognize mistakes, and results in an enlarged vision of the importance of the thing they are attempting to do. It is undergirding present co-operatives with an informed group of men and women who know what they are doing and why.

Past efforts at co-operation have not had such a foundation. The result was a host of mistakes which it is now possible to avoid. In previous years the reaction to failure was emotional—parties affected often became haters of the very name co-operative and simply refused to try again. Today the reaction is much more likely to be analytical and critical. It is not uncommon to find groups failing in their first effort, then re-examining their experience, and starting over again. Instead of blaming co-operation, they blame themselves for blundering—a much healthier attitude for co-operators to assume.

Affiliation of the younger wholesales and their local societies with the Co-operative League is helping combat the virus of over-expansionism. In this older organization are many men and women who remember well the hectic days of 1918 and 1919, when everybody was trying the chain-store idea and attempting to improve on Rochdale practices. They know the dangers involved in too rapid growth.

When lusty youthful wholesales started joining the League in 1933 these older voices were almost lost in strident marching calls which the new generation of leaders were sending out to the consumers of America. But as the novices have continued to wrestle with the practical problems of co-operative operation they have found it a sobering experience. The counsel of older heads is being listened to with sincere respect. Co-operative education is coming to include a critical examination of past mistakes.

As understanding of consumers' co-operation grows it cannot but help solve the problem of overlapping services. No co-operator talks intelligently about the movement without insisting that consumers are everybody. Men may not agree on politics or religion, they may differ in occupation, they may or may not be producers, but they must consume to live.

The consumer interest simply knows no barriers of race, class, creed, color, or occupation. That insight is leading some farm organization leaders to question the propriety of labeling co-operative societies with divisive names. It is creating a sense of common purpose among the rank and file of co-operators.

The growing membership of both the League and National Co-operatives are concrete expressions of the trend toward unity. In 1928 the League had fewer than 150 local societies affiliated with it. The largest group was the societies connected with the Central Wholesale at Superior. Finnish and Bohemian associations backed by a handful of strong organizations among white-collar workers accounted for most of the League's strength. The emerging rural movement was developing aloof and alone. There was little consciousness of unity among rural organizations themselves. Each one was carrying on without much regard for what others were doing. But this condition changes with great rapidity. Most of the large independent wholesales are now League members. One by one the Farm Bureau, Farmers Union, and Grange co-operatives come in. Those which have not yet joined are showing a very friendly spirit.

As the League binds the wholesales together in an educational federation, National Co-operatives unites them in a commercial organization. The present list of those buying through National Co-operatives includes: Pacific Supply Co-operative of Walla Walla, Consumers' Co-operatives Associated of Amarillo, Consumers' Co-operative Association of North Kansas City, Central Co-operative Wholesale of Superior, the Co-operative Wholesale of Chicago, Midland Co-operative Wholesale of Minneapolis, Farmers Union Central Exchange of South St. Paul, and Eastern Co-operative Wholesale of New York. To these should be added the following co-operative wholesales which are members of National Co-operatives by virtue of their membership in United Co-operatives, Inc.: the Farm Bureau Co-operatives of Ohio, Indiana, Michigan, Pennsylvania and Maryland; and the Grange League Federation Co-operative Exchange, Southern States Co-operative and the Farmers Co-operative Exchange. Recently the United Farmers of Canada was added to the list.

At the 1938 Congress of the Co-operative League steps were taken to bring the two national organizations closer together. Branch offices of the League have been established in Chicago in connection with the offices of National Co-operatives. An interlocking directorate insures co-ordination of activities and program.

The formation of national co-operative federations—educational and commercial—have always preceded the great periods of growth in those countries of Europe where the movement has achieved power. No one can study the history of co-operation in Denmark, Finland, Sweden, England, Italy, Russia, France, Belgium without being impressed by that fact. Isolated societies working alone have never made significant progress. National unity is important for the future of American co-operatives. This is in the process of being achieved today.

The growing educational program plus the increasing unity of the movement are likely to be bulwarks of strength in the lusty American development. However, the day of failures is not at an end. There will yet be local societies started only to be abandoned and buried with those which have gone before. But as the rank and file of co-operators become more intelligent, as the help and advice of experienced people becomes increasingly available to new groups, failures should become more and more rare.

But the thing which will do most to make the American co-operatives permanent lies wholly outside the movement itself. If the present atmosphere of disillusionment among farmers, laborers, and thoughtful people of other occupations continues, nothing short of a revolution is likely to stop the growth of co-operatives. If the hopes for a returning prosperity continue to be disappointed, the search for new ways of organizing business will be intensified.

Co-operatives were born of adversity. They have thrived only where continued need prepared the ground for them. That preparation has been going forward since 1920 in rural America and since 1929 in the great industrial centers. Two decades of tinkering with the so-called farm problem by two political parties have brought no lasting security to the farmer. As his faith in government aid shrinks, his resolve to do things for himself co-operatively grows. Ten years of effort by two presidents to get the country out of its industrial depression have been in vain. Weary of waiting, the disillusioned city dweller is beginning to follow his country cousin's healthy example.

American co-operatives have a new social and economic environment. The frontier, with its vast unclaimed stores of natural resources, is at an end. The United States is no longer a new country. The conquest of a continent is complete. She has come of age economically. Problems which once could be dodged by moving westward must now be solved at home. There are no free lands to which the disinherited flee. Rural youth can no longer go to the city and easily establish themselves in business or industry. There is little left except to take the resources at hand and work with others for the solution of common difficulties. A situation like that has not existed in the United States before. Economic necessity drives the co-operatives forward.

CHAPTER XIII

Co-operation and Capitalism

THE RECENT RISE of the consumers' co-operative movement in America has been accompanied by a great amount of rhetoric and oratory. It has brought forth a virtual flood of literature—for and against. It has been extravagantly praised as a middle road between Fascism and Communism; it has been called a peaceful, evolutionary, "Christian" method of building a better economic order. It has been enthusiastically damned as a threat against free enterprise, has been ranked with Socialism and Communism as a dangerous subversive influence.

Orators and writers on both sides of the controversy seem to have missed the basic fact that co-operation is simply a method of organizing business. It is not a middle road between Communism and Fascism; it is not Socialism or Communism for the reason that all three of these widely publicized *isms* depend on the use of the political state to achieve their ends. Co-operation is non-political in character as capitalism is basically non-political. Both represent techniques of organizing men and capital for the purpose of buying, selling, and manufacturing goods and services.

a little more buying power for the dollars he has managed to earn?"

The answer lies in the effects which the two methods have on the distribution of property ownership. Capitalism tends to concentrate wealth; co-operation makes for widely distributed ownership of property.

The reasons are simplicity itself. By its technique of giving the largest share of the earnings of industry to those who have the largest investments capitalism makes the rich man constantly richer, in comparison with his less fortunate neighbors. Two men may start out in the same corporation—one making an investment of $100,000 and the other $1,000,-000. If an average dividend of 10 per cent is received and all of it saved, at the end of ten years the difference between the wealth of one and the other will double. When they start, the richer will have $900,-000 more than his fellow. At the end of the period he will have $1,800,000 more. Under capitalism nothing can prevent a growing gap between rich and poor, between those who have little and those who have much. This tendency is inherent in the technique.

This is not to deny that circumstances may modify this natural result. The American frontier conditioned it for a long time. So long as there were great stores of unclaimed natural resources it was possible for some men to start with nothing and die rich. Nature placed rich treasuries of oil, gold, coal, timber, and iron at the disposal of those individuals who could claim them. In the race for them poor men sometimes got there first. In the days when men were hungry for machinery to make the world's work easier, poor men sometimes found friends who helped them exploit inventions which made them rich. But the percentage of men of wealth who rose from the ranks is less today than it was a generation ago. The frontier is at an end.

There is little disagreement about the fact of the growing concentration of wealth in America. The statisticians quarrel about the rapidity of the process but few deny that it is taking place. Small business men are being crowded out by chain stores, the independent farmer slowly yields ground before the land owning insurance company and corporation farming. The independent artisan loses out before increased mass production. This happens not because capitalists as a class are any worse or any better than the mine run of farmers, laborers, small business men, and professional people; it happens because, under capitalism, it is inevitable.

Control of wealth under capitalism is even more concentrated than ownership. It is easily possible for a business having 25,000 shareholders to be controlled by a single man. It is solely a matter of owning the necessary 51 per cent of voting stock. The creation of a holding company to own the 51 per cent makes concentration of control even easier to achieve.

The co-operative technique, in contrast to capitalism, makes for wide distribution of both wealth and control of business enterprises. Again, the reason is simple. A co-operative pays its earnings to its patrons—the largest single group of persons in direct economic relationship to it.

By way of example take a more or less typical co-operative handling farm supplies. It has 13 employees, 340 shareholders, and 1,500 patrons. During 1937 it made more than $4,000 with a capital investment of $8,000. Had it been an ordinary corporation it would have paid a common share dividend of more than 50 per cent. However, the shareholders received just 5 per cent in interest which was 10 per cent of the total earnings. The remaining 90 per cent was distributed to the customers. Those who were not shareholders received their refund in terms of share capital. Each year the organization adds about thirty people to its shareholding group who come in by the patronage dividend route. This three-year-old organization began with less than 200 stockholders. Every patron is a potential owner of a co-operative. As earnings improve with growing patronage the number who share in them inevitably increases.

Control is as widely distributed as ownership. The democratic principle applies. No holding company can get control of a co-operative. This is not to deny that with the consent of the majority a minority may exercise the franchise; but in any democracy there is no minority control which the majority does not accept of its own volition.

Capitalism by concentration of wealth creates conditions in which dictatorship and autocracy can readily flourish. Co-operatives, by distributing wealth to the consumers, make for the preservation of political and social democracy. There is no equality among men of widely differing degrees of wealth. Those who control a nation's wealth will eventually achieve control of its political and social institutions.

One need only read history and survey contemporary life to be convinced of that fact. Rome began its history as a democracy. When wealth became sufficiently concentrated the Caesars took control. Under slavery the slave owners' voices were heeded in the halls of government. Under feudalism the lord of the manor was ruler.

When slavery was dominant in the southern states less than 20 per cent of the population of the area owned slaves and yet the whole political policy of the Old South was determined by that 20 per cent. They finally led the entire population into war with the northern states in order to preserve the economic system which they cherished.

Under feudalism the lord owned the land, the mill, the smithy, and most of the services needed for simple manorial living. Likewise he was the judge and military ruler of the people. When the Christian church began, it was made up of propertyless people. The Christians were persecuted with impunity. In the course of time the church acquired property in its own right. It did this by persuading members to remember the institution in their final wills and testaments. When the church became the custodian of vast estates its prelates were listened to by political rulers. Their favor was sought and courted. Eventually the head of the church became more powerful than temporal rulers—but the power was rooted in temporal possessions.

As the Middle Ages progressed, trade began. The merchants of the towns made themselves substantial men of wealth by keeping the profits from lucrative buying and selling. In time the towns became free political units. Venice, Florence, Pisa, Genoa, Antwerp, Lubeck, Cologne, Danzig, were numbered among the self-governing cities of the Medieval centuries. Their people paid allegiance to neither manorial lord nor prelate of the church. In the course of events the merchants supported kings against barons, and nations grew.

Henry VIII was one king of this changing period. He is remembered in part because of the way he defied the church. He confiscated its lands and disobeyed its decrees. The thing that is forgotten is that he was the richest man in his realm when he made his defiance effective.

Finally the merchants defied the kings. They worked their will peaceably in England. The king became a figurehead. Democracy was established, but it was a democracy serving the imperial ambitions of traders and manufacturers. Autocracy could not have better promoted their ends. Democracy is tolerated when it serves the interest of property. If it threatens to serve other interests, those who own are perfectly willing to repudiate it.

Sometimes a group without property makes a mad bid for political power. Like children attempting too soon to exercise the prerogatives of adults, they are properly suppressed. Even the sinews of violent revolution are forms of wealth. The function of police and soldier is to protect life and *property*.

Back of the political upheavals of the past lay changes in the ownership of lands and factories. Politics today is as sub-servient as ever to economic forces.

This is true in nations; it is also true in villages. Look at any American town or city. The city council freely appropriates money to pave the boulevard that runs past the best residential property. It puts the best lighting system where the wealthiest live. A committee of business men is usually welcome in any politician's office. Representatives from the Minister's Association or the Trade Union may be given a hearing, but very often they are not heeded.

The running of schools and colleges is usually entrusted to men of property. They are sought out for school boards and to act as trustees of colleges and universities. They may not exactly determine what shall be taught. They do determine who shall teach, and the result is the same.

The churches claim a higher allegiance than the things of this world but they ordinarily manage to keep a working partnership with those who have earthly possessions. Virtue is often verbally exalted as a thing to be honored and desired above all things else. Practically, much virtue without property loses out in the contest with a little virtue judiciously associated with the proper amount of wealth. A recent tour of America was made by a group of outstanding clergymen for the purpose of "stirring the spiritual life." In every city they planned dinner meetings with the Christian business men. The idea came as an after-thought that there ought to be dinner meetings for Christian labor leaders. In the eyes of God there may be no difference between those who have and those who have not, but in the eyes of those who claim to speak for Him—property, like murder, will out.

Those who own, control. They are the determiners of the uses to which wealth may be put. If a man owns the sources of food he will feed himself first. If there is a surplus, he, if he is benevolent, will gladly extend to others the privilege of eating. If he is callous or indifferent he may not care. Or he may feed the hungry to still their cries in his ears. But it depends upon what he wants to do about it. If a man owns a factory he determines whether or not it shall run. No one tells him he must. If he runs it, it is only natural that he should consider its relation to his own welfare first. That men do this is not a sign they are depraved: it is a sign they are human.

The under-dog may deeply resent these facts. The moralist may deplore them; the philosopher fail to find them rational. The wise person will build according to them. To flout them is futile. It does no good to wish they did not exist or to declare they ought not to be.

Some of the politically minded try to thrust them aside. They seek security for the human race and the prerogatives of ownership through the ballot. They spend the major portion of their efforts trying to elect the right people or the right parties to power.

A desperate few strike with violence and then die martyrs to impossible causes.

The evangelist seeks to make saints of men and hopes thereby to make them perfectly obedient to the golden rule in their relations to one another. The world has known some saints. They have compelled its admiration; won its respect. And yet their way of life has been strangely neglected by all save a select and honored few.

The wise reformer keeps his program deeply rooted in the fact that property is the basis of kingship. Those who own, rule. Those who want a world in which the institutions of business, government, education, and religion are the servants of the people will be interested in consumers' co-operation simply because it is a technique of business organization which makes for wide distribution of wealth.

It is a good preventive medicine against the dangers of concentrated ownership of productive property even when a relatively small percentage of the total business flows through co-operative channels. What has happened in America in the field of petroleum products is an excellent illustration. The wholesaling of gasoline and kerosene to farmers was once a very profitable business. The first co-operatives which entered the field regularly paid from 5 to 10 per cent refunds on purchases. It was no uncommon thing for the entire capital investment to be repaid in a single year out of earnings. These conditions do not exist today. There has been steady lowering of the margins of profit until refunds paid by co-operatives in certain areas have shrunk to 1 and 2 per cent. But the whole rural population is enjoying substantially reduced prices. In some cases the reduction has been as much as three cents per gallon of motor fuel. The co-operative oil associations are still thriving but the profits made by old line companies operating in the field has been drastically curtailed. At present only about 15 per cent of the rural distribution of petroleum products is in co-operative hands.

Fertilizer furnishes an equally interesting story. For a long time this industry was dominated by a few large companies who dictated prices. Their practices finally called for a prolonged investigation by the Federal Trade Commission which has not hesitated to say that the fertilizer trust had practically squelched competition in the field. But today fertilizer prices are sufficiently low that the buying power of the farm dollar spent for this commodity is greater than in 1914. The Trade Commission attributes this to the growing power of farmer-owned consumers' co-operatives. The potency of co-operation in squeezing out excessive profits is shown by the difference between Ohio and Indiana as over against Kentucky prices. Until 1935 fertilizer was sold cheaper at retail in the Hoosier and Buckeye states than it was at wholesale in Kentucky. Ohio and Indiana had co-operatives; their neighboring state did not. And yet only 16 per cent of the fertilizer sold in Ohio and Indiana goes through co-operative channels.

It is not necessary that co-operatives control a third or a half of the business volume in any field before they begin to make impact on the capitalistic tendency to concentrate wealth. Through ownership of a relatively small portion of the channels of distribution and the means of production the consumers can put effective brakes on the abuses of economic power which go along with monopoly.

Capitalism and co-operation will probably exist alongside each other for many years to come. The growth of co-operatives will create a balance wheel in an economic system that seemed doomed to run unevenly because it could not control its own excesses. They will serve to checkmate attempts at monopoly, to narrow margins of profit, to lower prices, and to increase purchasing power. They will thus help stabilize employment long before they reach the zenith of their power.

As to how rapidly this corrective work is done will depend entirely on the consumers themselves. If they are ready to assume the responsibilities of carrying on business, co-operation is a technique by which they can effectively do so. If they want others to serve them for a price, the service will continue to be rendered on the capitalistic basis. If co-operatives grow rapidly it will be because the consumers divert their patronage from capitalistic channels. If capitalistic business grows it will be with the life-blood of the consumers' dollars. The patrons decide. No business can survive without a market. Nothing can stop a business which has the consistent support of an increasing number of buyers. The American consumer still has money enough to buy the kind of economic system he wants.

CHAPTER XIV

Consumers' Co-operation

As MEN FACE THE decisions which the present age places before them it is important that they realize both the limitations and strength of the consumers' co-operative movement as a program for improving economic conditions. There are some things it cannot do.

It does not offer labor an immediate defense against wage cuts, lengthened hours, and bad working conditions. Such protection can be secured only through efficient labor unions which enable the workers to bargain collectively and effectively with their employers.

It does not offer the farmer an immediate relief from low prices for his farm products. The farmers have largely left the marketing of their produce in the hands of others. They can expect little better treatment than they now are getting from commission houses and processors until they have set up marketing machinery of their own. Farmers must sell collectively to protect their prices. Consumers' co-operatives often work in close co-operation with farmers' marketing associations but they are not a substitute for them.

The movement does not offer the vast army of unemployed immediate relief from the hardness of their lot. Unless industry decides to take care of those whom it discards—which isn't likely—government will have to carry the burden of unemployment relief at the expense of those who pay taxes. There is no other choice.

Co-operatives have no way of organizing the political power of their members. They never dabble much in politics save in the interest of self-protection. They do mobilize occasionally to secure the passage of enabling legislation or to prevent the passage of bills aimed at their destruction; but they are not an important political influence. The election of public officials who believe in democracy and who will exercise the authority of government impartially and with due regard for the needs of all classes and conditions of men will require political organizations which begin in the precinct and end with a national party program. Consumers' co-operation is an economic, not a political movement.

But while it is not adapted to achieving these immediate ends there are other claims which it makes on the loyalty of the thoughtful consumer. It is the one program of economic action which asks men to organize themselves in the capacity in which the present owners of business flatter and cajole them rather than in the capacity in which they are reviled and scorned.

A producer asking for a better share of the world's income is met with hostility and coldness, a consumer with money to spend is welcome in any market place.

The efforts of workers to organize themselves for collective bargaining over wages and hours has met with violent resistance. Strike-breakers have been employed to inflict personal injury on men asking for better incomes. The power of police and National Guard has been used repeatedly to break up meetings of laborers. Organizers of unions have been beaten and imprisoned for trying to mobilize men for collective bargaining. The collective efforts of farmers to secure better prices, a larger share of the consumers' dollar, have met with indifference, ridicule, and hostility.

But when urban laborers or farmers become consumers with money to spend, all this is at an end. Courteous salesmen wait on the prospective purchasers. Clever advertising subtly invites them to buy. Stores create attractive displays to please the eye. Radio programs are hurled across the ether to tickle the ears; men and women with pleasing voices and polite manners court the buyers' favor. Those who will hire thugs to beat a laboring man for joining a union will likewise dismiss a subordinate that is discourteous to a customer. Whatever resistance is set up to the collective effort of laborers, farmers, and professional people to secure a better income for themselves, consumers are treated with all the pleasing arts that can grace human intercourse.

Even the organized consumer gets such treatment. There are on record some cases in which wholesales and manufacturers have refused to sell to co-operatives, but no organized consumer group has ever been permanently denied a source of supply for goods. The sellers always turn up. Today, with the volume of many of the co-operative wholesales in America running into the millions, salesmen crowd the waiting rooms of their offices. And in their dealings with the buyer of a co-operative wholesale these salesmen practice all the arts which the retail customer expects as a matter of course when a purchase is made. As consumers, human beings are treated as such.

The courtesy which businessmen show their customers often keeps people blind to the significance of consumer organization. They fail to realize the reasons for purchasers receiving such courteous treatment.

Business is hungry for markets. Those who own stores and factories know the power of the consumers' dollar. They know that success or failure in selling means life or death for a business enterprise. The profits they collect from the consumer pays for the expansion of their property—if they are successful. The good will of the buying public is the greatest asset of any man or corporation with goods to sell. Hence courteous salesmen, hence attractive advertising, hence beautiful store fronts, hence all the devices of modern salesmanship.

Consumers' co-operation alone offers a technique by which the exploited can use the thing which business wants most—their purchasing power—as a means of achieving a more satisfactory economic status.

It is also unique in that it tackles the present economic muddle at the point where capitalism has most conspicuously failed. There is no argument about America's capacity to produce. The Brookings Institute has amassed the evidence that, by full use of the present productive machinery and available man power, it would be possible to lift the standard of living of every American family by the equivalent of $1,000 per year. America certainly has not reached the saturation point in her capacity to consume. Despite all the talk about surpluses there is little excess of any consumers' goods. If the American farmers, industrial workers, and low-paid professional workers had the purchasing power, they would take off the market immediately enough manufactured goods to furnish work for a host of the present unemployed. Distribution has broken down. A spurt of manufacturing fills warehouses with goods but it does not place them in the hands of the consumers.

The industrial revolution has made the processes

of producing wealth essentially *co-operative*. The principle of mass production and division of labor implies co-operation between producers. Each man and group of men carries on a part of the process. In producing cotton cloth some spend the whole day tending spinning machines, others watch the power looms, still others dye and color. When the cloth is finished, it is cut and made into garments in another factory by another set of workers. A given number of men and women can produce much more clothing by working together, each doing a different task, than would ever be possible if each individual worker did all the various things necessary to convert a bale of cotton into dresses and shirts.

While the textile workers make shirts for farmers, farmers grow cotton from which the cloth is made and produce food for textile workers. Each occupation has its place in the picture.

The division of labor has become a matter of geography as well as occupation. Akron makes tires for automobiles produced in Detroit. Pennsylvania, northern Indiana, and northern Michigan specialize in iron and steel. Kansas and the Dakotas flood the nation with wheat. Iowa and Illinois produce a large portion of the corn and hogs of the country.

The day of interdependence is at hand. A breakdown in one section of industry affects other sections. A strike in one city may paralyze the business life of another. Production is co-operative. The system of distribution remains competitive. The average town has many more grocery stores than it needs and certainly more filling stations. Services overlap, duplicating equipment is maintained.

Consumers' co-operation starts with distribution in its program for changing the economic scene. It begins with the store and the filling station and works back through wholesaling to production and financing. It bids first for control of the channels through which goods flow to the consumers. It takes over production after its market is organized. It seeks to solve a distributive problem by reorganizing distribution itself.

It makes its appeal to human beings on the basis of the one interest which they have in common—their desire for more to eat, to wear, to wear out, and use.

Nothing is harder than uniting producers. The farmers of central and northern Wisconsin have sought to move their milk into the city of Chicago every time the farmers of northern Illinois and southern Wisconsin struck for higher prices. Maine potato growers have done their best to capture the markets of Ohio potato growers, in Cleveland, Youngstown, Cincinnati, and Columbus. Poultrymen of California seek the New York market of eastern egg producers.

The striking laborer always finds his greatest battle against fellow workers who are willing to take his job away from him. The American Federation of Labor never seriously concerned itself with the problems of those who work in the mass production industries until forced to do so by the competition of the CIO. Now the country is treated to the interesting spectacle of seeing two labor organizations sabotaging each other. Men quarrel and fight over how they should be organized as producers.

All men are consumers; that and that alone is their common economic interest. On the basis of it co-operation seeks to unite them for ownership of the means of distribution and the tools of production. It seeks to resolve the conflict between producers by uniting them as consumers. There may be another way of doing it but America has not yet discovered it.

Consumers' co-operation has little appeal to the political minded; those who still believe, like Robert Owen and the Christian Socialists, that the interests of the producer should be paramount will look on it with suspicion. Those who lust for class war and militant uprisings of the under-dog will regard it as a pale and colorless palliative. Those who think basic economic changes can be wrought overnight will desert it to follow those dreamers who promise bread and circuses tomorrow.

But those who understand the motives back of the flattering treatment given the consumer by present business leadership, those who realize that the root cause of present difficulties is choked channels of distribution, those who are truly desirous of seeing America become an economic brotherhood, feel differently. They are the ones who will give the present onward march of consumers toward co-operative ownership of business and industry its inspiration and its leadership. The organization and extension of consumers' co-operatives may not be the only thing needed to bring about proper distribution of the wealth America can produce, but it certainly is one of the things which is essential.

A century and a half has flown since *three Englishmen* started the industrial revolution which has freed so much of the world from the terrors of actual scarcity. The inefficient productive power of the muscles of men and beasts has been increasingly replaced with the tireless energies of machines. Never has the world known or visualized such possibilities for production as it has today. The real potentialities for abundant consumption were never so great. Poverty is largely a historical hang-over—accepted, not because it is necessary, but because it is a social habit. Nowhere in the world is it more unnecessary than in America. And yet it lingers on—a dead weight on the present, a threat against the future. A generation that could be free retains its shackles because it is accustomed to them.

Index